Library of
Davidson College

THE
WALLS OF CONSTANTINOPLE

AMS PRESS
NEW YORK

CONSTANTINOPLE FROM THE SEA OF MARMORA.

THE WALLS OF CONSTANTINOPLE

BY

CAPTAIN B. GRANVILLE BAKER

LONDON: JOHN MILNE
1910

Library of Congress Cataloging in Publication Data

Baker, Bernard Granville, 1870-1957.
   The walls of Constantinople.

   Reprint of the 1910 ed. published by J. Milne, London.
   1. Istanbul—Walls—History. 2. Istanbul—Antiquities, Byzantine. I. Title.
   DR729.B34   1975   914.96'1   72-178513
   ISBN 0-404-56509-3

914.961
B167w

Reprinted from an original copy in the collections of
of the Ohio State University Libraries

From the edition of 1910, London
First AMS edition published in 1975
Manufactured in the United States of America

AMS PRESS INC. 75-6537
NEW YORK, N. Y. 10003

PREFACE

ROMANCE and the history of walled cities are inseparable. Who has not felt this to be so at the sight of hoary ruins lichen-clad and ivy-mantled, that proudly rear their battered crests despite the ravages of time and man's destructive instincts. It is within walled cities that the life of civilized man began: the walls guarded him against barbarian foes, behind their shelter he found the security necessary to his cultural development, in their defence he showed his finest qualities. And such a city—and such a history is that of Ancient Byzantium, the City of Constantine, the Castle of Cæsar.

What wonder then that man should endeavour to express by pen and pencil his sense of the greatness and beauty, the Romance of a Walled City such as Constantinople. The more so that a movement is on foot to remove these ancient landmarks of the history of Europe and Asia.

True there are other works on this same subject, works by men deeply learned in the history of this

Preface

fair city, works that bid fair to outlive the city walls if the fell intent of destroying them is carried into execution, and from these men and their works I derived inspiration and information, and so wish to chronicle my gratitude to them—Sir Edwin Pears and Professor van Millingen of Robert College, Constantinople. There are many others too in Constantinople to whom my thanks are due—His Majesty's Vice-Consul, my host, his colleagues, now my friends, and many others too numerous to mention. They all have helped me in this work, and I am grateful for the opportunity offered me of here recording my thankfulness for their kind offices.

B. GRANVILLE BAKER.

NOTE.—As I have taken the historical events recorded in this book not in chronological order, but as they occurred to me on a tour round the walls of Constantinople, I have appended a brief chronological table, for the guidance of my readers and for the elucidation of this work.

CONTENTS

CHAP.		PAGE
I	CONSTANTINOPLE	13
II	THE APPROACH TO THE CITY BY THE BOSPHORUS	28
III	SERAGLIO POINT	54
IV	SERAGLIO POINT (*continued*)	84
V	THE WALLS BY THE SEA OF MARMORA	101
VI	THE GOLDEN GATE	124
VII	THE GOLDEN GATE (*continued*)	147
VIII	THE WALLS OF THEODOSIUS TO THE GATE OF ST. ROMANUS	172
IX	THE VALLEY OF THE LYCUS	198
X	FROM THE GATE OF EDIRNÉ TO THE GOLDEN HORN	225
	ENVOI	252
	APPENDIX	255

LIST OF ILLUSTRATIONS

CONSTANTINOPLE FROM THE SEA OF MARMORA . *Frontispiece*

Facing page

GENOESE CASTLE AT ENTRANCE TO BOSPHORUS FROM THE BLACK SEA 31

ANATOLI HISSAR, OR THE CASTLE OF ASIA 39

ROUMELI HISSAR, OR THE CASTLE OF EUROPE . . . 43

THE TOWER OF GALATA 51

THE LANDWARD WALLS OF THE SERAGLIO 58

THE PALACE OF HORMISDAS, OR JUSTINIAN 101

THE SEA-WALL 117

THE MARBLE TOWER 122

POSTERN WITH INSCRIPTIONS OF BASIL II AND CONSTANTINE IX 124

THE GOLDEN GATE FROM SOUTH-WEST 126

THE APPROACH TO THE GOLDEN GATE FROM NORTH-WEST . 146

YEDI KOULÉ KAPOUSSI, OR GATE OF THE SEVEN TOWERS . 170

PART OF TURKISH FORTRESS OF YEDI KOULÉ . . . 172

THEODOSIAN WALL AND APPROACH TO BELGRADE KAPOUSSI, SECOND MILITARY STATE 183

THEODOSIAN WALL—A BROKEN TOWER, OUTSIDE . . . 188

THEODOSIAN WALL—A BROKEN TOWER, INSIDE . . . 190

GATE OF RHEGIUM, OR YEDI MEVLEVI HANEH . . . 193

TOP KAPOUSSI, GATE OF ST. ROMANUS 194

THIRD MILITARY GATE 196

List of Illustrations

	Facing page
THE VALLEY OF THE LYCUS, LOOKING NORTH	199
THE VALLEY OF THE LYCUS FROM INSIDE THE WALLS	201
THE VALLEY OF THE LYCUS, SHOWING WHERE THE LAST EMPEROR FELL	224
THE PALACE OF THE PORPHYROGENITUS FROM THE FOSSE	226
THE PALACE OF THE PORPHYROGENITUS FROM WITHIN THE WALLS	228
TOWER OF MANUEL COMNENUS	232
GATE OF THE BOOTMAKERS, OR THE CROOKED GATE	241
WALL OF PALÆOLOGIAN REPAIR	244
TOWERS OF ISAAC ANGELUS AND ANEMAS	246
OLD HOUSE IN THE PHANAR	249

THE
WALLS OF CONSTANTINOPLE

CHAPTER I

CONSTANTINOPLE

Byzas the seafarer stood in the sacred copse, the copse of fir-trees dedicated to his father Poseidon. His soul was filled with awe, for he was listening for an answer to his prayer; he had prayed for help and guidance in his next venture out upon the seas, and had brought rich gifts with him.

Hush! the faint murmuring of the evening breeze—a sound—a whisper only—it is the voice of the Oracle: "Build your city opposite the City of the Blind, for there you shall prosper." The voice died away in the stillness of evening. Gently, with reverence, Byzas placed his offerings upon the ground, turned and went his way without looking behind him.

Before the dawn arose, Byzas had joined his comrades. "To sea," he cried, "for the Oracle has spoken thus: 'Go to the Country of the Blind—there

The Walls of Constantinople

build you a city opposite their own—you shall prosper.'" Silently the stout vessel that carried Byzas and his fortunes stood out to sea as the rosy dawn touched the high peaks of the Peloponnese and tinted with pale carmine and gold the unruffled water of the Ægean. And ever bearing to the north, to that unknown region, with Byzas at the helm, the ship held on. They sounded here and there, and asked of those they met, "Is this the Country of the Blind?" Their question met with little sympathy; the answers are nowhere recorded. After many vain inquiries the adventurous crew drew out into the Sea of Marmora. Towards evening they sighted land.

No doubt Byzas was drawn towards the Prince's Islands 'twixt him and Asia as he sailed northward up the quiet inland sea. But sternly he resisted the temptation of these lovely isles, and held on his way. His long craft pulled nearer in towards the narrow mouth, and through the twilight a great city loomed up before him on his right—the city of Chalcedon, better known by its modern name of Kadekeuy. Now in the days of Byzas suspicious-looking craft of no ostensible occupation were not encouraged, piracy was too common and, indeed, considered one of the few occupations fit for a gentleman—night was falling; so we imagine Byzas putting in to the spit of land that

Constantinople

projects boldly into the sea as if to meet the Asiatic shore and offer stepping-stones for any migrant Titan that might pass that way. Rounding the point, he saw before him a broad waterway winding inland till lost to sight behind the tree-clad heights to northward. So Byzas steered towards this fairway, holding to the southern bank, and then, some little distance from the point, his comrades lowered the broad sails, dropped anchor and awaited the light of day. Only when it dawned were they conscious that they had reached their goal, the country mentioned by the whispering Oracle.

A fair sight that, by the first rays of the rising sun: the east aglow with many colours, repeated in the waters of the winding bay, henceforth to be known as the Golden Horn; first touches of pink in the small clouds over the rose-tipped mountain of the East; and, swimming in a silvery haze, the islands they had passed.

Then the keenest and most fleet-footed of the crew betook themselves ashore. They searched diligently everywhere, and brought back word that all day long never a man had they seen of whom they could inquire, "Is this the Country of the Blind?" So Byzas spoke: "This is the Country of the Blind, for those are blind who could pass by this most favoured spot, and build their city on the other side."

The Walls of Constantinople

So Byzas settled here and built a city and prospered—the Oracle had spoken truly.

All this happened many centuries ago, when the world, at least the Western World was young, and Rome—Imperial Rome, the eternal city, was still wrapped in the legendary mysteries of her birth.

And so arose Constantinople,—a city known by many names, the one familiar to the majority of those of Western race is that of the City of Constantine, Constantinople, familiar but with subconscious charm of strange remoteness: the Slavs still talk of Tsarigrad, the Castle of Cæsar; to the Turk this is Stamboul, a corruption of εἰς τὴν πόλιν—the phrase they must have so often heard on the lips of the vanquished Greeks, but through all ages this is Byzantium in romance. The first thing a man does when he comes into any kind of property, is to safeguard it somehow. If this property be land, however acquired, the natural thing is to build a wall around it, and this no doubt Byzas did too. But of his walls nothing is left—the city grew and prospered, the Oracle said it would, so the matter was in a sense already settled, and new walls were thrown out further until Imperial Byzantium, like Imperial Rome, stood on seven hills.

Behind these walls a busy populace increased the wealth and importance of the place, and others who

Constantinople

wanted wealth and importance flocked in here for it. Byzant became a thoroughfare to all those of the West who did business with the East, but was chary of being too much of a thoroughfare for those who came from the East. For these latter had the habit of coming in swarms and armed, otherwise empty-handed, but with a sincere wish not to return in that condition. Against such as these the walls were built, strong and cunningly planned. And so ancient Byzant grew into the mart for those who traded from the West along the coasts of the Mediterranean, away through Dardanelles and Bosphorus to the Black Sea, to Trebizond, where the old Greek tongue yet lingers in its purest form, the Crimea—even distant Persia. So also Byzant became the bulwark that met, and broke, successive storm-waves of Asiatic attack, until in due season a strong Asiatic race forced its way in, and has stayed there, and still holds its hard-won stronghold.

It was this position that made Constantine, the man of genius, transfer the capital of his empire from Rome to Byzant, after defeating his rival Licinius at Chrysopolis (Scutari) opposite the mouth of the Golden Horn, and henceforth to make the city known as his—Constantinople, the Castle of Cæsar. This alone would justify his claim to be called Great, and, as Dean Stanley remarked, of all the events of Constantine's

The Walls of Constantinople

life, this choice is the most convincing and enduring proof of his real genius.

It is to be doubted whether any city walls have such a stirring history to relate as those of Constantinople, except perhaps the walls of Rome. Of former, older fortifications traces have been found, and they reach back to very ancient history.

Echoes come to us from those dim ages of history, shadowy forms of warriors, seafarers, priests and sages pass by in pageant, with here and there the bearer of some great name in bolder outline. Somebody has said that the East is noteworthy as the grave of monarchs and reputations. Of no spot is this truer than it is of Stamboul.

Chroseos, king of Persia, emerges from the gloom, and with him hordes of warriors trained to ride, to shoot, to speak the truth. He is seen for a brief space encamped before the walls to bring its citizens to submission : he fades away with his phantom host. Then comes one better known, and he stands out in bold relief, the light of history gives him more definite outline,—Pausanias. He drove the Persians from the city after defeating them in the field. His handiwork, 'tis said, can still be traced in some gigantic blocks that went to fortify yet more the walls that Byzas built. He was recalled in disgrace : well for him had he never

Constantinople

come. It needed but a little of the splendour and luxury of an oriental court to corrode the old iron of the Spartan character. For him the watery soup and black bread of the Eurotos valley could never have quite the same flavour afterwards. He left the city a discredited politician of more than doubtful loyalty to the land that reared him and the great confederacy which had set him at its head.

Then follows an everchanging array of warriors of many nations, many races. Seven times did the fierce sons of Arabia, fired by their new-found faith, lay siege to old Byzantium, and seven times their impetuous valour broke against these walls in vain. Albari, Bulgarians, Sclavi, Russians, vainly spent their strength in trying to force an entrance into the Castle of the Cæsars. Great bloodshed or great treachery could alone serve as the key to what latter-day poets call "the Gate of Happiness." Crusaders too, men of the same faith, besieged the city, and after one short period of success, they too vanished, to leave the imperial city standing as before; to leave her, perhaps, a little wickeder, perhaps a little more luxurious, but still as perennial and unchanging as she is to-day.

Then came another, stronger race out of the East. They laid their plans cunningly and boldly executed them, they hovered for years over the city and around

The Walls of Constantinople

it, and for years their efforts proved abortive, until the time had come when this bulwark of Europe, that had for centuries hurled back the waves of warriors that dashed themselves against its ramparts, had fulfilled its mission. Vain it was to cry for help to the Christ whom they had persistently dishonoured, and to whom their very existence, corrupt and luxurious, was a standing insult. No, they in their turn were compelled to make way for the stern realities and honest animalism over which the Crescent cast its protecting shadow. Then did the conqueror Mohammed enter into possession, he and his people; here they settled after centuries of storm and stress, and here they are still, and they too are prospering—as said the Oracle in those dim distant ages before the Greek seafarers landed here.

Meantime, behind those sheltering walls, Europe was working out its destiny.

The Western Empire centred in Imperial Rome succumbed before the on-rush of barbarians from the north, those warriors from primæval forests, blue-eyed and strong, whose very aspect reduced the stout Roman legionaries to tears of terror and despair, with fair hair floating in the breeze as their long boats (sea-serpents they called them) bore them from shore to shore, or as astride o their shaggy horses they

Constantinople

crossed the frontiers guarded by Roman legions, and conquered as they went. Then these took root, the Langobards in northern Italy, Goths in the Iberian Peninsula, Saxons and Angles in Britain, and, by degrees, became conscious of political existence.

Some vanished before the fury of the Arab as did the Goths in Spain, while others grew and prospered like the Franks. Races emerged from darkness to add to the confusion of Europe's seething mass of humanity. Christianity shed its light upon them, and by degrees order appeared, to make way again from time to time to wild disorder.

And all the time the walls of Constantine's proud city prevented the irruption of any Eastern foes whose advent would have made confusion worse confounded.

So on the eastern frontier of the eastern empire a wonderful revival of the power of Persia was held in check by those who held the fort of Constantine, and a vigorous attempt to regain the possessions of Hellas-hated Xerxes was frustrated.

Transient states arose and vanished—the republic of Rome, the exarchate of Ravenna, mythical Celtic kingdoms like Armorica and Cornwall, and the Vandal kingdom of Africa. Thereupon appeared the more lasting dominions of the Moors at Cordova and Granada, and of the Normans in France

The Walls of Constantinople

and Sicily, and the enduring Power of the Papal See.

Slowly, uncertainly, under the shelter of the walls of Constantinople, Europe drew the first rough outline of her present political aspect, and began to emerge from barbarism.

Ambitions and strange freaks of fanaticism flared up among young nations and died away. Among the former the revival of the Roman Empire by Germanic monarchs lingered longest. Conceived by Charlemagne with the aid of the Roman pontiff and his own paladins, this dream lived on for many centuries, caused endless bloodshed and such cruel deeds as the murder of that hapless Conradin, the last of the Hohenstauffens, a race of rulers that had given rise to many legends and heroic lays. Then the Crusaders with all their fruitless sufferings, their lavish shedding of blood and treasure, and the masses of private iniquity which they died trusting to expiate by public sacrifice.

And yet Constantinople held the eastern foe at bay. The tradition of Rome's all-conquering legions lingered yet, and old Byzantium boasted of a standing army, highly trained and disciplined through all these centuries—those stormy times for Europe, when every man's hand was against his neighbours. Then

Constantinople

bands of armed men roamed over Europe, following this leader or the other, each bent only on his own advancement.

Little by little degeneration set in within and without the walls of Constantinople. One fair province after another was regained by those barbarians from whom they had been conquered, and the mighty Eastern Empire fell to pieces. The spirit of the people was no longer bent on upholding the traditions of the past, or, mayhap, lived too much in those traditions.

So when the nations had begun to settle, the day of Constantine's city was over and its task accomplished. The eastern foeman achieved the oft-attempted end, and possessed himself of those ramparts which so long had kept him at bay, and established a new empire in place of the vanished power of Roman tradition. There is yet another aspect to the history of Constantinople. It was here that its second founder embraced Christianity. St. Sophia and St. Irene still stand as monuments to mark that happening, albeit the crescent, not the cross, now glitters from their pinnacles ; although portly, bearded Imams now take the place of the long-haired Greek priests, and the high altars have been turned awry, so that the faithful may know that their gaze is fixed direct towards Mecca.

The Walls of Constantinople

Here much of St. Chrysostom's life and energy was spent; here, since the schism with the Church of Rome, has been the Seat of the Patriarch, head and high priest of the Greek Church.

Rulers, dynasties, even governing races have replaced each other, yet here the Patriarchate still maintains the dignity of the great Church it represents. For the strong man who vanquished this proud city did not seek to turn his new subjects to his faith, but rather gave them full liberty to follow their own. And this has been the policy of his successors; thus it is that a Greek patriarch, Joachim, third of that name, this day watches over the interests of his flock. Adherents to every creed, save that of the Armenians, have enjoyed complete religious freedom, and Jews who were hounded out of Catholic Spain took refuge under the Chalif of Islam.

The same policy is continued by those clear-headed men who have but recently revived the Empire of the East, and trust in time to give it a government conceived on modern lines. Romance! Are not the pages of history, even the most recent, made glorious by it? So who will deny the attribute of romance to the story of a walled city?

Think of the enterprise, the ingenuity, the steadfast endeavour that led to the encircling of ever-increasing

Constantinople

areas within the embrace of those stout walls; of the life of the people who pressed onward out of paganism to Christianity, from despotism to constitutional government.—Romance!

In younger days wars were waged because some fair lady had been carried off, some rich jewel stolen, and in order that black insults might be wiped out. We live nowadays beneath a more sombre sky. From isolated incidents our motives have crystallized into definite principles, and it needs the delicate eye of the artist to see any of the old lustre in our honest if humdrum efforts to defend them.

Constantinople—the name conjures up dreams of Eastern colour, Eastern sights, and Eastern smells: visions of Turks in baggy breeches and jaunty fez; visions of bearded elders in flowing robes and turbans, white, green or multi-coloured according to the wearer's calling, descent, or personal taste, for only he who is learned in the Koran may wear white. Those who claim descent from the Prophet bind their fez with green, and divers colours are worn more by Ottoman subjects from over the water. Then you dream of stalwart sunburnt Turkish soldiery whose bearing speaks of Koran-bred discipline and stubborn fighting, and a fanaticism which takes the place of imagination. Gorgeous cavasses, frock-coated followers of Islam with unshaven jowls and green umbrellas, smart Bedouins and copper-coloured eunuchs from Abyssinia, immaculately-attired dragomans, veiled ladies, more mysterious even than their Western sisters—in fact, splendour, squalor, light and life, and all as picturesque and romantic as dreams can be. This is the vision, and the reality to whosoever is fortunate enough to see Constantinople is its fulfilment. All but the dragomans, perhaps, for you may pass one by and not know he is that wonderful omniscient being—a dragoman. He will hide his greatness under a straw hat, maybe, he may even affect an air of Western hustle.

But every other effect makes up for any disappointment one may experience over dragomans. In a golden haze kaleidoscopic changes, every type of face a study, every street corner its own distinctive character, even the spick and span liners that lie along the quays, or have their station in the fairway of the Golden Horn, seem to adopt a catchet other than their register provides for them. Over all, the domes of many mosques with their attendant minarets, from which the call to prayer goes forth, they point the way to the goal of all good Moslems, and few there are who allow this world's cares to interfere with their devotions. Later in the day these mosques, silhouetted in the gold of a Stamboul sunset along with the other tall columns

Constantinople

"qui s'accusent" against the sky, go to form, as Browning (who had never seen them) suggests, a sort of giant scrip of ornamental Turkish handwriting.

So, having followed this sketch of Constantinople's history from Byzas to these days, in which an almost bloodless revolution has been accomplished, let us approach the city, and mark the bulwarks that are left, and hear what those massive towers and battlements have to tell us.

CHAPTER II

THE APPROACH TO THE CITY BY THE BOSPHORUS

AUTHOR and Artist have, for the sake of compactness, been rolled into one. This method leaves to both a free hand and ensures absolute unanimity: their harmonious whole now proposes to the reader a personally conducted tour around the walls of Constantinople, within and without, stopping at frequent intervals to allow the Artist to ply his pencil while the Author holds forth to an eager circle of intelligent listeners.

Constantinople should not be approached by those who hail from the West with any Western hustle—no charging to the agents or the booking-office at the last moment to demand a return ticket by the quickest possible route, to traverse all Europe, passing through many strange and interesting countries with the determined tourist's reckless haste, to tumble out on to the platform of the German-looking Stamboul railway station, worn out and wretched and wishing to be back at home again. Rather should the traveller wean his

Approach to the City by the Bosphorus

mind from many Western notions. Let him disabuse himself of the hackneyed superstition that time is of any moment. In the East it is not. Men have all the time there is, and plenty of that. In this respect it corresponds to the biblical description of Heaven: "There is no time there." Conscious of their easily won eternity, trains, and more particularly boats, make no attempt to start at the hour mentioned in the schedule, aware that by doing so they would only cause inconvenience to the large majority of their passengers. Any one who has had official relations with the Turk knows that his most frequent exclamation is "Yarsah—yarsah" ("Slowly—slowly"), but to most foreigners the system is, at first, a little disconcerting. Again, the traveller should prepare his mind for what he hopes to see—a walled city,—so should, ere starting, let his mind's eye travel beyond his garden wall, against which perchance he may safely lean as aid to meditation, to what he has heard of walls, walls that were built by many devoted generations and in return protected their descendants from those hungry powers that seek to destroy whatever prospers.

And travelling toward his Eastern goal the reader passes through many an ancient city whose walls chronicle the history of its inhabitants. He should take his journey easily, should move eastward with no undue

The Walls of Constantinople

haste. Let him go down the Danube, that mighty river which arises from a small opening in the courtyard of a German castle, flows majestically through the lands of many nations, where before the days of history Saga held her sway and gave birth to the Nibelungs. In its waters many ruined castles are reflected, amongst others Dürnstein, where Blondel's voice at length brought hope of deliverance to his imprisoned liege, Richard Cœur-de-Lion. He will pass many fair historic cities, Vienna, Budapesth, Belgrade, the White Fortress, and so on through the Iron Gates, whence the great stream swells with increasing volume through the plains of Eastern Europe to throw out many arms to the Black Sea. It is here that Author and Artist await you; for to worthily approach Constantinople you should do so from the north, and by sea. And you are in good company, for by this seaway came the Russians in their several attempts on the Eastern capital. The Turks, too, the present masters of the situation, found this way and followed it to victory. These, too, overcame great difficulties—they sailed in small vessels and were much at the mercy of wind and weather; in fact, the Russians found their plans frustrated by the elements. They met with anything but a pleasant reception, whereas the traveller nowadays steams in great comfort in a racy-looking Roumanian

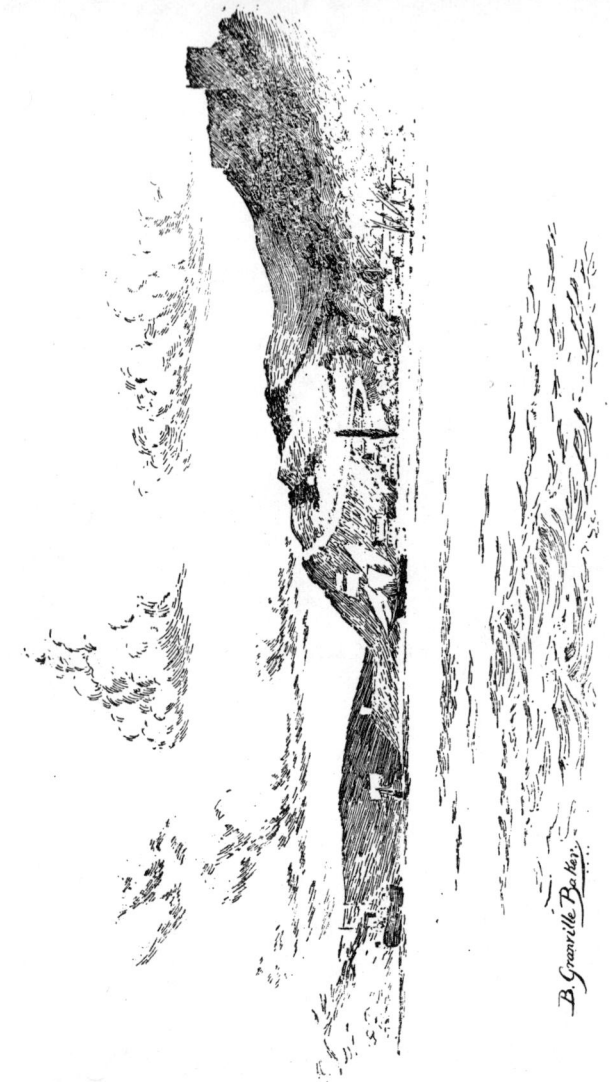

GENOESE CASTLE AT ENTRANCE TO BOSPHORUS FROM
THE BLACK SEA.

A narrow entrance this—strongly fortified it was too, in olden times, for on that height to the left stands a frowning ruin, a Genoese Castle.

Approach to the City by the Bosphorus

liner, and is sure of a courteous welcome from his hospitable host, the Turk.

Along the coast of Bulgaria—that kingdom of strong men under a strong ruler, whose history, with a long and melancholy hiatus, is taken up again, is in the making, and bids fair to rival that of older nations as a record of devotion and steadfastness of purpose. And so to the mouth of the Bosphorus, a narrow entrance through which the strong current of the Black Sea forces its way to join the warm waters of the Mediterranean.

The Argonauts found their way through here, braved the crash of the Symplegades, and sailed out into the unknown in search of the golden apples of the Hesperides. Let no man say that these were simply oranges, for these a man may cull in many a Greek garden to-day. No—it was an ideal they sought, and, like true men, they found and followed it.

A narrow entrance this, and strongly held, as it deserves to be if Nature be man's handmaid. Strongly fortified it was, too, in olden times, for on that height to the left stands a frowning ruin, a Genoese castle, commanding the entrance for many miles round the open sea and the rolling, wooded heights of Asia inland.

Intensely interesting are the naval exploits of the city republics of Italy during the Middle Ages. It is

The Walls of Constantinople

not easy to realize the power developed by such towns as Pisa, Genoa, and Venice, and the enormous importance of the part they took in the development of Europe. Other cities are so much overshadowed by Rome, that those who are not historians hear only echoes of their greatness.

Primarily there seems to be a divergence in the origin of empire between those gained by a northern or southerly race. Latin empires grew out of cities—Rome and Constantinople, and Athens with her Delian Confederacy; the States of Pisa which owned large oversea possessions, Genoa which to a long strip of coast counted Corsica among her spoils, Venice which with varying fortunes controlled Dalmatia and Istria and built the stout fortress of Nauplia commanding the Gulf of Argolis. Whereas England, France, Germany, in fact those empires founded by the men of a Northern race, began, it appears, by the conquest of other people's cities, and, making themselves masters of a number of such towns, started states of their own, drawing liberal and very elastic boundaries round them which they could enlarge when strong enough by the simple expedient of picking a quarrel with their neighbours. These depended for their defence more on those who lived in fortified seclusion on the marches of their domain than on the town-dwellers.

Approach to the City by the Bosphorus

The Genoese navy, composed of ships fitted out alike for battle as well as for commerce, was free to look further afield as soon as Pisa, their whilom ally against the Saracens of Africa, Spain and the Mediterranean islands (but a formidable rival at all other times), had been finally crushed at Meloria. Opportunity soon offered, for trouble arose as usual in the Eastern Empire. The Latin dynasty put into power by the crusaders was sinking lower, and a feeling for the restitution of the Greek Empire was growing. Also, the Venetians, new rivals, had assisted the Latins, so there was every reason to interfere. The interference proved successful, Michael Palæologus conceded the suburbs of Pera and Galata to the Genoese. These places were fortified, and served as a base from whence to push Genoese enterprise further into the Black Sea, and in the Crimea a factory was established. From time to time the Genoese turned against the Greeks, no doubt in order that their swords might not rust for want of exercise during the piping times of that peace which in the East was a seldom acquired taste. They stood by the Greeks, however, when trouble came from elsewhere, and to the last upheld their high reputation for bravery and devotion.

The Genoese tower of Galata still stands overlooking the Golden Horn. A yet more notable monu-

The Walls of Constantinople

ment to those gallant seafarers are the so-called "Capitulations." The Genoese colony was ruled by a magistrate sent from home, and to this day that right is still granted to the Powers of Europe, and can only be fully appreciated by those familiar with the ordinary standards of Eastern justice.

On the next height the Giant's Mountain, also on the left bank, is another monument of yet greater antiquity, though perhaps its historical value is less easily assessed—depending more than ever on personal opinion and a romantic nature completely undisturbed by the galling limitations of probability—the Tomb of Joshua. Its origin is shrouded in mystery, as it well may be considering the countless ages that have passed over it—there are so few records of Joshua's travels that no doubt that eminent warrior may have gone on leave to travel for the improvement of his mind like his colleagues of the present day without our hearing anything of his experiences in foreign parts. It is equally possible that he may not have returned from furlough —owing to decease. This is purely speculation—very real, however, is the tomb itself. A long, narrow, walled-in space in connection with a small mosque and under the care of the Hodja in charge contains this, his resting-place, enclosed by iron rails and about 24 ft. long by 10. It also serves as fruit garden, or

Approach to the City by the Bosphorus

orchard—for several fig-trees grow here, so we see that, unless the legend lies, Joshua must have been a tall strapping fellow and the sons of Anak can have caused him no real surprise or alarm.

The correct thing to do is to walk round the tomb a great many times (there is a fixed number, but it does not matter much), tie a bit of rag to the railing and express a wish, keeping it strictly to yourself. The next best thing to do is to forget the wish, pay twopence in baksheesh and ride away to get the most of a glorious view. Artist and Author alike do so.

And a pleasant thing it is to ride on into Asia Minor on an alert, sure-footed Arab; he need be surefooted, for at one time your road leads along the very edge of a steep decline, at another over the bed of what is a rushing torrent in the rainy season. Everywhere a changing vista, bold, rolling hills, now covered with short scrub and heather, with black rocks peering through it—now under oak and beech, everywhere the glorious bracing air of the uplands mingled with breezes from the Northern Sea. Here and there you find patches of cultivation, the patient team of oxen drawing the primitive plough, merely an iron-shod staff at an angle to the shaft to which the team is yoked. Near by, a village, small wooden houses sheltered by fig-trees, a little shady café where of an evening the

The Walls of Constantinople

men smoke a solemn hubble-bubble and discuss events in the measured sentences of a conversation which begins about nothing in particular and ends in the same district.

What changes those fields have known! armies pouring into Asia full of enterprise and the lust of conquest, returning to escort a victorious emperor in triumph through the Golden Gate, or beaten remnants of a host to seek refuge behind the city walls. And a plough of the same construction, drawn by the same faithful servants, stopped its course a while to watch, and then went on its way unchanging.

But the fairest road is still that glittering waterway with its ever-increasing number of craft, so we pass on to Constantinople. With a fair breeze from the Black Sea dead astern small sailing vessels hurry on towards their goal—the Golden Horn. They are high in the bows, higher still in the poop, with an elegant waist but withal a reasonable breadth of beam, brightly painted too, with cunning devices on the prow and sails that glisten white under the Ottoman ensign; they carry for a flag a crescent argent in a field gules (the Artist insists on heraldic terms, as they are so picturesque). These little ships have been busy collecting many things for the Stamboul market along the Black Sea Coast. Heavy-laden tramps thump onward to

Approach to the City by the Bosphorus

Odessa to return with corn or wool. We overhaul a yacht-bowed Russian mail-boat and get a shrill whinny of greeting from the stout little passenger steamers, Tyne-built, that ply between the many landing-stages along the Bosphorus bringing officials, business men and even artists back from the city to those quiet, cosy little bungalows that hide among the trees on either side. White-painted caiques flit across from side to side, one-oared and even two-, some more pretentious ones with more oars still, the boatmen dressed in becoming uniform, veiled ladies in the stern sheets. A hustling steam-pinnace shoots by from one or the other "stationaires," for every larger Power keeps one here; and there on the right, that row of gleaming palaces by the waterside is Therapia, those palaces the different embassies in their summer quarters. Here homesick travellers of many nations may feast their eyes on the war-flag of their country and get up a thrill, if the scenery should have failed to cause one. It certainly is a pleasant sight to see a sturdy British bluejacket again or his smart colleague of the U.S. Navy in his jaunty white hat. Therapia will tell you that this is the only place to live in during the summer; other places along the road on either hand claim the same advantage, and the claims must be allowed where the choice is so difficult. For there is Candilli, and who that has spent some sunny weeks under the trees of that favoured spot, has dived from the garden wall (displacing volumes of water) into the evening phosphorescence of the Bosphorus, but wishes to return and to repeat the performance? And Arnoutkeni, where, on a hill-top, lives the most hospitable of consuls-general.

The silvery way narrows and widens, and winds, though slightly, past ever-increasing signs of human habitation. Wooden Turkish houses with the jealously latticed windows of the harems dipping their stone foundations in the sea, some with a little scala leading to a stoep, where the veiled ladies of the house may take the air while children play around them. Stately palaces walled off towards the land, the sea-front open and mayhap the lordly owner's steam-yacht moored just opposite, barracks and cafés with vine-clad trellis-work, and behind the narrow stone streets and little shops. Every now and then a mosque, its dazzling minarets pointing to the sky, and also, too frequently, a very modern residence in the very latest bad taste, which is saying a good deal.

To all this a background of trees, the warm depth of pines, the pleasant green of oaks and beeches, the bright shining green of fig-tree, and everywhere larger or smaller groups of slim cypresses, close-serried beneath whose shade rest faithful sons of Islam—and

ANATOLI HISSAR, OR THE CASTLE OF ASIA.

Within the precincts of this castle, entered by narrow gates, are other small houses, still smaller shops and cafés.

Approach to the City by the Bosphorus

surely none of them might wish for a more lovely and decorous burial-ground than here, looking out upon the narrow strait their fathers won so dearly.

There are open spaces too, where groups of people, gay patches of bright colours, disport themselves: a game of football is no unusual sight here. Even a factory chimney stands out here and there, not emphatically belching out defiant volumes of black smoke to insist on the power of the *main-d'œuvre*, but in a gentler manner, as if rather apologizing for this outrage upon nature and trying its best to adapt itself to its surroundings by the kindly aid of quaint-looking craft, blackavised, but free from any suggestion of machine-made regularity; these craft carry the coal necessary to enterprise, just to oblige, they seem to say.

The Channel widens, then narrows again, and here stand two ancient fortresses, one on either hand. Ancient, compared to Western notions, though too recent to be mentioned by chroniclers of Old Byzant, for they are of Turkish origin, and date back but a few odd centuries. On the Asiatic side stands Anatoli Hissar, or the Castle of Asia. Wooden houses of all ages cluster about it, the wood of some painted in bright colours, pink or ochre, or others left to be coloured by time and climate, ranging from warm purple greys to the strongest burnt Sienna. Within the precincts of

The Walls of Constantinople

this castle, entered by narrow gates, are other small houses, still smaller shops and cafés. To southward broad green streams join the Bosphorus, the sweet waters of Asia, along the banks of which are pleasant open spaces, a mass of colour on Friday afternoons; for here the Moslem ladies take their leisurely walks abroad on that day, and spend many pleasant hours chatting under the shady trees, though what they find to talk about except their children, Allah alone knows. The bridge leading over the northern arm of these waters in an attractive spot: here the Artist put up his easel to sketch the continuous stream of passers-by—grave merchants, portly of person on small donkeys, small horses laden with baskets, pedestrians many and of all manner of races, mostly Eastern, now and again a squad of cavalry on active little Arabs, or a body of infantry with the fine decisive tramp of a conquering race. At the foot of the rather high-arched wooden bridge a number of caiques, white-painted with crimson cushions, their oarsmen dozing in the sun, while heavier boats laden with fruit and vegetables go out to market at Stamboul. Across the bridge quaint wooden houses with the usual latticed windows, and, connecting them across the narrow street, vine-covered trellis-work beneath the shade of which some business is transacted, buying and selling conducted with all the leisure and

Approach to the City by the Bosphorus

decorum of men for whom a year more or less means little. Behind and crowning all, the frowning though dismantled fortress. Here the Artist had an experience that struck him enormously. His morning sketch was of the scene described above, his afternoon work was from inside a boat-builder's yard, looking over the sweet waters to some Turkish houses, glorious in colour with quaint wood carving, each with its tiny well-kept garden by the sea.

The second day while at work on the morning sketch, the genial boat-builder approached and confided the key of his establishment to the Artist, at the same time intimating that the yard would otherwise have been found closed and thus the afternoon's sketch delayed. Would this have happened on Clyde or Tyne?

Over against Anatoli Hissar stands Roumeli Hissar, the Castle of Europe, a yet more imposing mass of ruins. Its plan is said to be the cypher of Mohammed. The whole fortress is said to have been built in two months by the forced labour of Greeks, to each of whom was delegated a measured area. The towers that command the upper part are of the construction peculiar to the Turkish architecture of that period, a tower of smaller dimension superimposed on the lower one is what it looks like, and we shall see it again at

The Walls of Constantinople

Yedi Koulé. This castle encircling a picturesque village is peculiarly beautiful in the spring, for then the flaming colour of the Judas tree, swamping with its vivid tone the delicate pink of almond sprays, lights up the deeper ochres and purples of the surrounding masonry, and makes the dark cypresses that stand all about strike even a yet deeper note than when the glamour of high summer bathes all things in a golden haze and draws light even from these sombre trees. And they are so beautiful, though perhaps a bit wistful also—their slender shape, the warm grey and purple of their stems and branches and the cool depth of their foliage.

Close by this castle stands Robert College.

Further south, obliquely opposite is Candilli, a place where it is good to be. At first glance, but for its prominent situation, it may appear to be much like other places along the banks of the Bosphorus. A short bit of narrow street, stone-paved and very bad to walk on, leads to a cross-road, the cord that connects all these little villages. It is equally badly paved, but as many of the blocks of stone that once served as pavement have vanished, there are quite a number of softer spots wherein a man may set his feet when walking. There is a café by the waterside, where Turks, Armenians, Greeks and others take their

ROUMELI HISSAR, OR THE CASTLE OF EUROPE.

Over against Anatoli Hissar stands Roumeli Hissar, the castle of Europe. Its plan is said to be the cypher of Mohammed.

Approach to the City by the Bosphorus

leisure, drink endless cups of coffee and gaze into the water.

The gentleman who sells tickets to those who leave by boat, and collects them from those who land here, may generally be seen fishing from the landing-stage. He is a philosopher; it is but little that he wants, and he takes a long time getting it. There is a mosque close by whose Hodja is counted among the Artist's personal friends. He is a busy man, as Turks go: he sweeps out his mosque, trims and lights the candles that adorn it by night, and fulfils all the Koran's requirements in daily prayer, encouraging others in the same commendable practice. He also possesses a magnificent tenor voice which is heard to best advantage rising up from his minaret to the hill overlooking Candilli, when exactly one hour and a half after sunset he announces to the world that "Allah is Great. There is no God but Allah, and Mohammed is His Prophet." He has a son who is learning to chant the same refrain and to quote the Koran. Like most of the early apostles, he is a fisherman.

All around by the seaport, on the hillside, in garden and under trees, stand the houses of those who live in Candilli, either permanently or as summer tenants only. Should the reader ever visit here, let him turn sharp to his right and keep along the sea-

The Walls of Constantinople

front, a stone-paved terrace about 8 feet broad occasionally broken to admit boats into the boathouses, caverns in the stone foundations of the houses that stand here. These breaks are planked over for the convenience of foot-passengers; and so we keep on till a sharp turn to the left takes us to a flight of steep steps. We ascend and join the high-road, the cord referred to above. You are welcomed there by a sportive litter of pariah pups who have an *al fresco* lodging here on a luxurious bed of melon-skins, which provide food and bedding at the same time, and quite a plentiful supply of each during the season. The neighbourhood for miles round, city and suburbs, is full of little corners convenient for receiving things that you no longer want. A few hundred yards along the high-road another sharp turn to the left, another litter of pariah pups and their white mother, generally called the "old lady," all most pleased to see you; another ascent, short but sharp with holes torn out of the pavement as if the shell of a cow-gun had struck it, and you arrive at a doorway in the wall. It is quite unpretentious, in fact its modesty is carried so far that a piece of string that dangles out of a hole will, when you pull it, lift the latch and so give you admittance.

You enter an unpaved yard, in fact after a few days' rain you may call it a garden, for grass grows up with-

Approach to the City by the Bosphorus

out any other encouragement, just as it does in all Eastern gardens. Before you stands a wooden house, shrouded with vine and overshadowed by a fig-tree; there is yet another fig-tree in the garden, and a walnut-tree and another sitting-out-under tree, which finds that sufficient avocation, and therefore yields no fruit of any kind.

Entering the house, the first thing that meets your eye and holds it is a row of boots on the left-hand side of a stone-flagged apartment called the hall. Your eyes rest on the boots, for you know at a glance that they are British made—they are, for Englishmen live here. A doorway opposite the entrance leads to the kitchen; here the Greek cook, Aleko, reigns supreme, and with him the butler, Kotcho, which being interpreted means Alexander and Constantine. A wooden staircase leads to upper regions, to a spacious sitting-room, where no one ever sits save in wet weather. But why this lengthy description of an ordinary English bachelor abode ? the reader asks of the Author. He gets behind his collaborator—the Artist lived here, and thus history is made.

The Artist lived here as the guest of those whose work lies in Constantinople. There were several, their numbers had frequent additions towards the week-end, and the assembly went by different names, the most common being the "Y.M.C.A.," because one of the number nearly lunched in the company of a bishop one day, and a bishop in the Levant is rare enough for comment.

They lived in great contentment, did these Britons abroad; at work during the day, they foregathered at dinner in the variegated garb that betokens ease and talked of many things between the peals of the pianola wafted from a villa higher up on the hillside. They listened to the Eastern sounds that came to them from afar, to the warning hum of the mosquito, the distant barking of a dog, the tapping of the watchman's iron-shod staff on the pavement outside. One night they heard his cry of "Yungdin Var" ("There is a fire"), as in accordance with time-honoured custom he proclaimed some distant conflagration, while his colleagues all along the coast on either side gave the same warning. This call sounded in the lane below the bungalow, and was vigorously repeated from within. The watchman answered, "Pecci, pecci, effendi" ("All very fine, gentle sirs"—or words to that effect), but tell me where it is? and then himself announced the place and went on his way rejoicing in a "score."

Now and then these men would sally forth of an evening to one or the other hospitable house, to dance or dine, a solid phalanx of dazzling shirt-fronts.

Approach to the City by the Bosphorus

The nights on the shores of the Bosphorus are very fair. Quite still, the lights of Stamboul and Pera gleaming in the distance, the swish of passing steamers whose searchlights flash unbidden through your windows, and the moonlight reflected in their wash in myriads of sparkling facets. And then the rosy dawn dispelling the faint haze upon the waters, when the tall trees that are silhouetted black against the clear nocturnal sky, lose their sharply-defined shape as they resume their colours and merge with the glorious scheme of awakening chiaroscuro.

And for many ages night on the Bosphorus has enjoyed this deep repose, making an occasional disturbance such as happens where men inhabit seem incongruous. Imagine the deep stillness when Byzas first settled in his City, set out in early morning to search out the land on his own side of this broad waterway, that led to lands remotely known to him through legend only. His constant pleased surprise at finding more and more treasure beautiful and material in the wooded bays where safe anchorage offered. And his return at nightfall in the stillness till he saw the ramparts of his City purple against the evening sky, faint lights twinkling and fainter sounds reaching him across the water betokening the activity of his settlers.

The Walls of Constantinople

These peaceful waters have known much strife and turmoil, the valleys on either hand, the hills of Europe and Asia have echoed back the sounds of battle. Fast sailing ships brought swarms of adventurers down time after time to try their fortunes before the walls of Cæsar's Castle. From Roumeli Hissar, the fortress built by Mahomed the Conqueror, right down beyond Seraglio Point and into the Sea of Marmora stretched that monarch's fleet. But it was of no avail against the seaward walls. Entrance to the harbour was impossible, as a chain had been stretched across the mouth of the Golden Horn, and behind it the larger vessels of the Genoese and Venetians rode at anchor. So Mahomed conceived a plan bold and in keeping with his character and ability. He decided to convey a portion of his fleet across country to the upper reaches of the Golden Horn and to attack the walls that guarded the upper harbour.

There appears to be some doubt still as to the exact spot where these galleys were beached and as to the route they took. Galata, the Genoese fortress, must be avoided, and at the same time the shortest route must be taken. Galata stands in a position somewhat similar to Constantinople, on a promontory formed by the Hellespont on one side and on the other by the Golden Horn, which bends slightly to the north after

Approach to the City by the Bosphorus

passing west of where the land-wall of Theodosias joined the sea-wall of the Bosphorus, towards the sweet waters of Europe. At any rate we pass the place where this great feat was accomplished, and this is how it was done. Mahomed made a road of smooth planks covered with grease, and along this road a host of men pulled eighty galleys in the night. The next morning these ships were riding at anchor in the upper, shallower part of the harbour beyond reach of the larger vessels of the Genoese and Venetians. According to the Byzantine chronicler Ducas, every galley had a pilot at her prow and another at her poop, with the rudder in his hand, one moved the sails while a fourth beat the drum and sang a sailor's song. And thus the whole fleet passed along as though it had been carried by a stream of water, sailing, as it were, over the land.

Certainly a most remarkable feat carried out to the sound of the drum. The drum an instrument, some say of torture during the month of Ramazan, for it serves to arouse the faithful Moslem an hour before sunrise that he may eat—for he may touch neither meat nor drink between sunrise and sunset during this fast, and it cannot fail to wake others in the neighbourhood. Entirely oriental in its origin—no doubt an ancient, its enthusiasts think venerable means of

The Walls of Constantinople

producing sound—its appearance in Europe is of comparatively recent date; in fact, not till after West and East met in the Crusades did the drum become part of a European army's outfit, and to this we may directly trace the creation of military bands, for where would any band, save a German one performing in England, be without a drum? We may conclude that in all probability it served a double purpose, the uncanny noise both struck terror into the heart of the enemy and cheered on "the Faithful" to battle. The Roman armies sounded the tuba, Frank or Teuton put his soul into a bullock's horn, which a later period imitated in brass, and that so successfully that not even the best of modern composers can altogether do without it. The Crusaders rallied their bands by means of horns, each in a different key, no doubt; the Saracens beat drums to draw their followers to the Crescent standard, and a happy blending of these two, with the addition of some attempts at harmony, now brighten the soldier's life when marching to church in sections, or returning heavy footed from a field day.

The traveller is at liberty to choose any spot he likes, given that it be on our right, to settle where Mahomed's galleys left the waters; that safely accomplished, he should look before him. We have passed many charming little villages quaintly named—Beyler-

THE TOWER OF GALATA.

Galata's proud Tower comes into view, and right at its feet the Golden Horn, all life and bustle and glittering harmonies of colour.

Approach to the City by the Bosphorus

bey, the Bay of the Beys; Tshengelkeui; Beshiktache; Kabatache. On the heights above palaces, palaces on the sea-front, as we sail on towards Constantinople, and there it is before us.

We see Seraglio Point, and then the view increases, showing a glorious vista of mosques, gleaming domes and tapering minarets. We pass on our right a couple of steam-yachts, bright and trim, moored opposite a splendid palace. H.M. the Sultan's yachts lie here, and his residence is the Palace of Dolma Bagche. On the heights above Pera, the city of Italian origin, now inhabited by those Western by birth or inclination, and standing some distance away from it, is Yildiz Kiosk, the deserted haunt of baleful associations.

Galata's proud tower comes into view, and right at its feet the Golden Horn, all life and bustle and glittering harmonies of colour. The very smoke rising from the tall funnels of tramps and ocean liners catches the light, reflects it, and add another beauty to the aspect.

Over our port bow we look down the smooth, shining expanse of the Sea of Marmora, in which the Prince's Islands seem to float as in a sunny haze. These have their history, and sad it is for the greater part, and reference will be made to that later, when the Artist has finished talking about the scenery, and

The Walls of Constantinople

has returned to his legitimate occupation. Behind these islands are faintly seen the mountains of the Asiatic mainland, then the coast draws in towards the Golden Horn, and here are Modar and Kadikeui, villages so called, though perhaps more truly suburbs, wherein you may find many hospitable houses. One of them gave shelter to a Turkish gentleman, a high-placed personage whom an angry soldiery were in search of during the last counter-revolution, the last dying effort of reaction. And here below Modar lie many yachts, for it is a fair sea for yachting is the Sea of Marmora, and the coast and the islands offer ever-varying change of scene. Then close to Kadikeui and north of it is Haidar Pasha, with its blot upon the landscape, the terminus of the Bagdad railway, an edifice German in construction and of consummate ugliness. Close under this eyesore is a peaceful spot where many tombstones and a monument bear record of the deeds of the English soldiers, victims of the Crimean War. A peaceful spot, and oh! so beautiful. Above it stands a large yellow building many storied, with a background of tall cypresses in thousands that shade the Turkish cemeteries, where many lie who fought side by side with Britons and our gallant friends the French against their old northern enemy, Russia. This building may fall to ruin and perish, the dead that lie about

Approach to the City by the Bosphorus

here and their deeds may be forgotten by all but the straight-stemmed cypress-trees, but the memory that lives about this place will never die, for it tells the glorious story of a noble woman's work—this building was Florence Nightingale's hospital.

And near here another work by women is in progress, work devoted to rising generations at the American Girls' College.

The traveller may cast a glance backward to the way he came and see a small tower standing in the sea —this is a trim-looking tower and shows a light o' nights—this is called the tower of Leander.

But no more looking back. We have arrived opposite Seraglio Point, and our goal is before us; for here is the starting-point of the strange and glorious history of the City of Constantine, here the foundations of the city of Byzas were laid—here is Constantinople.

CHAPTER III

SERAGLIO POINT

PERSONS of importance like our travellers land at Seraglio Point instead of travelling round to the bridge of Galata. Byzas did so, we have it in black and white a few pages back, so it must be true. We can without much fear of contradiction suppose that Constantine the Great landed here also, though perhaps he went to one of the harbours on the Sea of Marmora. Indeed, he is more likely to have done so, for the current runs pretty strongly and the sea is more than a little choppy at this point. Byzas had no harbour to turn into except the Golden Horn, and he must have been too eager to land and survey his new property to have followed that waterway any considerable distance. Just a little west of the point is perhaps the best place to land, somewhere near the Turkish Custom House.

It is, of course, very interesting to land at the bridge of Galata, passing through crowded shipping on the way up the Golden Horn. On one hand, to the south, one sees the irregular mass of buildings,

Seraglio Point

mosques, and public offices which go to form Stamboul. You may descry that vast square of solid ugliness owned by the international creditors of the Ottoman Empire and known as the Public Debt. Close by you catch sight of the head-quarters of Government—the Sublime Porte. Drowsy fox-hunting squires, to whom their wives read the paper of an evening, must often have started at the reiteration of this familiar phrase, and wondered to what year the marvellous Eastern vintage belonged.

Opposite the business quarter of Galata, crowned by its tower. The life, the colour ever changing, on the highway across the Golden Horn is extraordinarily fascinating. Sons of every race and nation upon earth are freely mingled here. The Western official or the business man, whose garb is allowed to betray no ease or originality, here brave the fierce suns of summer clad in the drab discomfort of business attire, with the Perote or native of Pera and Levantines of European origin who have imbibed some longing for oriental display without the requisite taste. Western ladies unveiled, Eastern ladies veiled, the latter in many cases beautifully shod and gloved. Also the Artist raves about a little hand he has seen ungloved, such a dainty, beautiful hand, and according to his own estimate he is an expert in such matters. Then there

The Walls of Constantinople

are Turks, Western Turks, whose costume is also Western, the fez and seldom-shaven cheeks being the only things in which they differ from others, for many are fair and most are fine, handsome men with every sign of the self-control good breeding gives. Hamals, the porters, push their way with backs bent double and their packs joined upon the leather rests provided for that purpose. Great men in carriages drawn by dashing, spirited Arab steeds roll by you, a servant in gorgeous livery beside the driver on the box. Asiatics of all kinds and colours, fantastically yet harmoniously clad, move past with silent, unhurried footsteps. And then a batch of soldiers, fine, upstanding fellows in business-like khaki, march past on their way to embark for the Yemen, the Sierra Leone of the Turkish Empire, for which men even volunteer nowadays, since the bad old order changed.

But we have landed our travellers on the northern extremity of the promontory on which stands Constantine's ancient city. This part serves as a public promenade, and here people take the air, admire the glorious view, and generally behave like people do everywhere else, when they find time for a leisurely stroll, the only difference being that here men find time for one more often. The point is open to the sea, for there is no further occasion for the walls and

Seraglio Point

towers that encircled this the starting-point of Byzantine history. Here was the first settlement of Byzas that grew into an Acropolis, walled, and strongly held, the heart of a growing empire. So we go inland, crossing by a bridge the railway that discreetly hides its unloveliness in a cutting before running into a terminus that might have been picked up from one of the Hanseatic towns and planted here by some malignant fairy.

The road leads upwards to the Seraglio buildings, and here is much of interest. There is the Museum containing many treasures, among them two of wondrous beauty—two sarcophagi, one of which claims to have held the remains of Alexander the Great, the other is presumed to be the last resting-place of one of Alexander's higher officers, and is known as "Les Pleureuses," from the beautifully-sculptured female figures in mourning garb that adorn it. Within these precincts is the School of Art, where much good, earnest work is being done under the guidance of Humdi Bey, to whose efforts the recovery of the sarcophagi and other monuments is due as the result of excavations in Asia Minor.

A broad road leads us with park-like plantations on either hand up from the sea towards the Seraglio buildings. These buildings stand on a height, the

The Walls of Constantinople

first of the seven hills that form the immovable foundations of the city.

The Seraglio no longer serves its original purpose, the Imperial Museums and School of Art have taken up a considerable portion of them, and others find accommodation for troops. Here you may see the stalwart Anatolian peasant being made into a soldier after the German pattern, and a very good pattern too. Bugle-calls, reminiscent of those heard in Germany, tells the Turkish soldier the time for all the many duties he should attend to. Sergeants in manner emphatic and teutonesque impart the mysteries of that solemn, high-stepping march which takes the place of route marching in an army that has to train its men to reach perfection in two years' time. Slim-waisted subalterns, whose moustaches follow Imperial precept, superintend these operations, and an anxious company commander may be seen in conference with his colour-sergeant.

It would sound invidious, it would savour of interference, to wonder which is the better use for the Seraglio buildings, that of the present or the past. The Artist doth profess loudly on this point, that no building can serve a higher purpose than that of housing in comfort those who are taken from their homes to learn how to defend the honour of their

THE LANDWARD WALLS OF THE SERAGLIO.

Romance and mystery cling to the place and live in the name Seraglio. It is jealously walled in, the wall being of Turkish construction and comparatively recent, and to it may be seen clinging quaint wooden houses.

Seraglio Point

country, and that again the honour and glory of a community is well served by making ample provisions for the encouragement of art. Both Author and Artist wish these Seraglio buildings a glorious future in their present warlike and peaceful missions.

But romance and mystery cling to the place and live in the name Seraglio. It is jealously walled in, the wall being of Turkish construction and comparatively recent, and to it may be seen clinging quaint wooden houses.

No doubt Byzas dwelt somewhere about here, though the exact spot is possibly beyond the ken of the keenest archæologist. Remains of solid masonry, huge blocks of stone, have been discovered near the Seraglio kitchens, of which a fine view is offered from the railway, peeps of the massive, high-standing building through the ranks of its solemn escort of cypress-trees.

When Byzantium became the City of Constantine it was found necessary to extend the enceinte of the older fortifications, as the number of inhabitants had grown prodigiously, and this first rampart was of greater extent than the present Seraglio walls. The many improvements made by Constantine, the palace he built unto himself, the Forum and Hippodrome he laid out, and the churches he erected, are nearly all within the immediate neighbourhood of the Seraglio,

The Walls of Constantinople

if not inside its precincts. So here again was the centre of the civic and religious life of the city, rising rapidly to the zenith of its power, and here it has remained until most recent times.

There were walls and towers round the point to guard the city both against her enemies and the violence of the elements, and, sooth to say, it was the latter caused more damage than the former. These had need to be constantly repaired. Of the very earliest walls no trace remains, yet they too had their page in history. Not far from where our distinguished travellers landed, just round the eastern point and looking east, is Top Kapoussi, which means cannon-gate, for here stood a gate dedicated to St. Barbara, who is the patron saint of gunners. But a more likely reason for the Turks to retain the memory of the original name is that close by stood a magazine or military arsenal when they conquered the city, and may have stood for years after. It seems that there was a yet older gate at this spot, a gate through which the Spartan admiral Anaxibius entered the Acropolis when he escaped from the city by boat along the Golden Horn, what time Xenophon and his truculent Greeks were in possession.

After Constantine had led his people, or at least those under his immediate influence, into the fold of

Seraglio Point

the Christian community, many churches sprang up about this northern extremity of the promontory. (There are, no doubt, those who will differ from the Author on the subject of Constantine's conversion, who may say that his people led Constantine to adopt Christianity, and that reasons of policy rather than the conviction born of a sudden inspiration guided him, but the Artist will on no account allow such a prosaic version.) Five churches stood about here, one dedicated to St. Barbara, as we have seen, another to St. Demetrius, a third to St. Saviour, yet another to St. Lazarus, and a fifth one built to St. George on the highest ground available just there, according to custom, for in former times all churches dedicated to the warrior's patron saint were built on higher ground, as if to give the saint an opportunity of keeping a good look-out from his sanctuary. This church gave to the Sea of Marmora its mediæval name of Braz St. George.

There were evidently other buildings in connection with St. George's Church, a monastic institution most probably, for here under the name of Joasaph the Emperor John Cantacuzene dwelt in seclusion after his abdication until he withdrew altogether from among his former subjects to a monastery on Mount Athos. Another great feature of this neighbourhood was its holy well, which may be springing still, though for

The Walls of Constantinople

this the Author cannot vouch, as he has not seen it. The Church of St. Saviour guarded this holy spring—its water had healing qualities, and pilgrimages were made to it on the Festival of the Transfiguration.

The life of the capital of an empire stirred the precinct of what is now the Seraglio enclosure and the vicinity outside it for close on twenty centuries. We have seen the city rise under the fostering care of Byzas its founder, and followed those dim paths of remotest history when the world was young, though no doubt the sad young cynics of the period thought it as old and foredone as they do to-day. Then came the glorious epoch of Constantine and his successors—glorious indeed in the new light of Christianity, but in that name much evil was done, and by it murder and violence and civil war were held to be excused. But through it all the city, this seat of empire, exhibited a most astounding elasticity and power of recovery. True the Palace of Cæsar built by Constantine was not within the precincts enclosed by the Seraglio walls of to-day, but the brain of the empire held its sway hard by here, and its tumultuous heart beat everywhere among the ruins and decay that now mark the site of palaces.

Constantine in his glory and genius passes, and others follow him in an unbroken sequence, some good, many bad, all human, and thus surrounded by the

Seraglio Point

romance that envelops those that played their part in history and did their share in making it. A noble sequence taking them all in all from Constantine, who reigned from 306 to 337, then his successors down to the last emperor, another Constantine of the house of Palæologus, twelfth of the name who fell before his city walls to be succeeded by a conqueror of the house of Ottoman, the house that has filled the throne of the Eastern Empire until to-day.

If we take but a few of this unbroken line of sovereigns, more than one hundred altogether, such names stand out in the world's history as Valens, whose aqueduct still stands as a monument to perpetuate his name. Then Theodosius II, whose master mind gave to the city its furthest limit in those proud walls that have encircled it since the beginning of his reign, and still stand as testimony to the genius of man. Justinian the Great, too, first of that name of whom we must say more when we come to the ruins of the lordly palace he inhabited. Leo V the Armenian who entered the city as a poor groom, they say, but served his Imperial master, Michael I the Drunkard, so well that he then ascended his throne and restored the expelled Government of the Empire. And there are many others of whom mention will be made elsewhere in connection with fortifications and palaces

The Walls of Constantinople

that were erected far beyond the first narrow limits of the city that Byzas had founded and the great Constantine made his own.

About this neighbourhood centred the life of the city; there was a broad esplanade near where the Church of St. Lazarus stood, down by the Sea of Marmora, its site probably not far from the foot of the Seraglio kitchens. This esplanade was called the Atrium of Justinian the Great, for it was his creation. And a fair place it was, all built of white marble. Here the good citizens might walk and breathe the soft air, looking out towards the Prince's Islands and the coast of Asia, across the Sea of Marmora, reflecting in its translucent depths the glorious colours of an Eastern sunset. And here they walked and talked, and no doubt discussed all subjects upon earth, religion, politics, those chief incentives to resultless argument, and the news, with all its variations, which were nothing uncommon even in the days before a daily paper first appeared. How portly burghers must have smiled with satisfaction at the sight of bellying sails that drove their galleys back from the shores of many countries to the great market.

Or a racing craft under full sail with all its rows of glittering oars rising and dipping in strict accord would round the point into the Golden Horn, leaving

Seraglio Point

the gazers in the Atrium the prey to many conjectures, until a gentle sound coming from the north, round by the Senate, growing to a roar conveyed the news of some great victory.

Perhaps an anxious heart of mother, wife or sister would beat against the coping of the Atrium, as tearful eyes followed the swift sails of departing war fleets that pressed onward into the morning. And the sun would rise to arouse the golden glories of the city, and yet leave that heart unlightened.

Here, too, good folk would meet to discuss the pomp and splendour of the escort that had brought the Emperor's bride-elect to the sea-gate of Eugenius down by the Golden Horn. How Cæsar there had met her with great pomp and ceremony, and had himself invested her with the insignia of her exalted rank. The talk would then go on to the high doings at the palace, and all those good things that had been brought together from every quarter of the earth for the delectation of the wedding guests. When lowering clouds obscured the brightness of the sun of Cæsar what whisperings, what anxious glances out to sea! Yes, and perhaps what black looks when an alliance was proposed, and indeed consummated, between a princess of their royal house and the polygamist ruler of their enemies the Turks, Amurath I.

The Walls of Constantinople

What troublous times and discontents when every messenger brought news of fresh disaster, of yet another portion of the Empire torn from its enfeebled grasp. What grumbling at the supineness of the Christian world that looked on with apathy when it could find the time to spare from its own internal quarrels, while the most Eastern bulwark of the faith was being hard pressed by those who carried Islam with fire and sword wherever they went. And then a ray of hope when as a last resource John VI Palæologus betook himself to Rome to implore the Pope to exert his influence on behalf of his expiring fortunes, and to stir up another crusade among the nations of the West. Though at the same time the Emperor sent one of his sons to serve in the Turkish army and learn those secrets of success which that host alone seemed to know.

Intrigue flourished at Constantinople more perhaps than anywhere, unless it be in Rome, and we well imagine how rumours of such matters filtered down among the populace, giving rise to conjecture and wild, inaccurate statements, the food that intrigue fattens on, rumour also of private feuds and family dissensions not only among nobles and leaders of the State, but among its lowliest citizens. So when John Palæologus betrayed his weakness and the weakness of his Empire, many among those who walked the Atrium

Seraglio Point

of an evening might search their minds for some one who could save them from the threatening devastation, and would gladly turn to any who promised to strengthen the shaky edifice and re-establish that sense of security without which all private enterprise was crippled. For here, as in the time before Saxon England fell to the Duke of Normandy, the conqueror's influence permeated, and attachments were formed between the highest of both nations.

So Andronicus, another son of John Palæologus, entered into friendship with Saoudji, one of the sons of Amurath. Saoudji was jealous of the favour shown to Bajazet, his brother, and resented the latter's popularity—well deserved too, for he was valiant and successful in the field, and through the rapidity and vigour of his charges acquired the epithet of Yilderim, or Lightning.

So while Amurath was away in Asia, Saoudji and Andronicus, with the assistance of a band of Greek nobles and retainers, organized a combined revolt against the Byzantine and Turkish Governments. Amurath got tidings of this, and forthwith recrossed the Hellespont.

Suspecting Palæologus of complicity, Amurath compelled him to join in his proceedings to quell the revolt. The rebel forces were encamped near the

The Walls of Constantinople

town of Apicidion, and Amurath marched against them.

Unattended and under cover of night he rode to the entrenchments of their camp and called aloud to the Turkish insurgents, commanding them to return to their allegiance, promising a general amnesty. All these on hearing the familiar voice deserted their new leader and their Byzantine allies, and rejoined the forces of Amurath. Saoudji and Andronicus with his Greek followers were speedily taken. Saoudji was brought before his father, who commanded first that his eyes should be put out as unworthy to look his last upon the day, and then that he should be slain. The Greek insurgents were tied together and flung two or three at a time into the Maritza, while Amurath sat by until the last was drowned. The fathers of some of the rebels were ordered to slay their children before him; those who refused were themselves destroyed. Amurath ended by sending Andronicus in fetters to his father, commanding him to deal with him even as he had dealt with his own.

And after all the suppliant Emperor's journey to Rome failed to arouse the Western nations to undertake a new crusade. All that was achieved was a confederacy to resist the future progress of the Ottoman power, and if possible to dispossess it of its

Seraglio Point

European territories. The Sclavonic nations, at the confines of whose territories the Turks had arrived, joined together at the instigation of Servia. Servians, then the best troops and the most formidable the Turks had met in Europe, Bosnians, Albanians and Bulgarians, and with them Magyars and men from Wallachia took the field. Though at times successful, the alliance failed eventually in its purpose, and not until most recent times have those nations emerged from Turkish suzerainty to national independence.

The Battle of Kossova broke the power of the Sclavonic race in the Balkans and led to their disappearance from the arena of the polity of nations for many centuries. A fierce fight it was that raged all day with varying fortunes and glorious display of chivalry and knightly daring, where Bajazet the Lightning struck swift and sure, though a Christian noble ended the conqueror's career when the fortunes of the day had just turned in his favour.

It happened thus, one Milosh Kabilovitch galloped forth as if a deserter from the Servian ranks and sought the royal presence of Amurath. He alleged important intelligence concerning the plans of the allies. Kneeling before Amurath, he suddenly leapt up and by one stroke buried his dagger in the monarch's heart. By a miraculous exercise of strength

The Walls of Constantinople

he beat off all the attendants who surrounded him again and again, but finally fell under the sabres of the Janissaries just as he had reached the spot where he had left his horse. Amurath survived but to the close of the battle. His last act was to order the death of the captured Lazarus, king of Servia, who had commanded the centre of the Christian force, and who, standing in chains, regaled the dying eyes of his conqueror.

News of this momentous happening reached Constantinople, and we can guess that the faces of those who frequented the Atrium grew gloomier. Was there no one who could help? The horns of the Crescent were closing in on the City of Constantine, the Empire was shorn of most of its former glory and its vast possessions. Little but the city and its immediate surroundings were left unsubdued, all escape from the conquering Turk seemed hopeless. And then what were their prospects? to be conquered, and by such ruthless hands! The death of Saoudji may have been reckoned an act of justice, but rumours came to them, and proved true, of other deeds more cruel, of how Bajazet ascended the throne, like Richmond on Bosworth field, of how his brother Yakoub, who had fought valiantly in the Battle of Kossova, and had contributed largely to its success, was summoned to the regal tent

Seraglio Point

and there saw his father's body, the first intimation of his death. How then and there in the presence of that body Bajazet had immediately ordered his sorrowing brother to be strangled. This act was done, says Seaddedin, the Turkish historian, in conformity with the precept of the Koran, "Disturbance is worse than murder." Surely a gloomy outlook for the watchers on the wall.

But how awful would be the fate of their city which had so long resisted the sacred Scimitar of Ottoman! What mercy could they expect? Help there was none, and Bajazet was making preparations to submit Constantinople to yet another siege. But he was diverted by hostilities on his western frontier, and hope revived again in the hearts of those that looked over the city walls across the Sea of Marmora. For the Christian natives of the West had at last begun to realize the danger threatening them from the East. They were moved not by the recommendation of a heretic Greek emperor, but urged by the supplications of the King of Hungary, a spiritual vassal of the Roman See. Pope Boniface IX proclaimed a crusade against the Turks, and promised plenary indulgence to those who should engage in an expedition for the defence of Hungary, and the neighbouring Catholic States.

The Walls of Constantinople

There were fewer sinners in need of indulgence in those days than there are now; but the population of Europe was proportionately smaller. Yet many rallied to the banners of Philip of Artois; Comte d'Eu, Constable of France; Vienne, Admiral; and Bourcicault, Marshal of France. The Count of Hohenzollern, Grand Prince of the Teutonic order, led a force of Germans; the Knights of St. John of Jerusalem, led by their Grand Master Naillac, joined the force of some 120,000 allies, all, as Froissart says, "of tried courage and enterprise." Their aim was to break the power of Bajazet in Hungary, and when this was done to advance on Constantinople, cross the Hellespont, enter Syria, gain the Holy Land, and deliver Jerusalem with its Holy Sepulchre from the hands of infidels.

How anxiously those citizens of Constantinople must have longed for news of the enterprise, how hope revived as the fall of Widdin, Orsova, and Raco were reported. What a heavy time of waiting it must have been while the Christian host lay before Nicopolis. Still hope held on, for Bajazet was in Asia, and was never expected back. But suddenly he appeared within six leagues of the Crusaders' camp. The news was brought in by foragers, and the impetuous French knights, sitting at their evening meal, at once buckled on their arms, and demanded to be led against the

Seraglio Point

foes. Against the advice of Sigismund of Hungary the French charged impetuously. They charged and broke the ranks of the Akindgi, the advanced guard of the Janissaries and of the heavy regular cavalry, and pressed on till they encountered the main body of the Turks under the command of the Sultan himself. Meanwhile the disordered ranks of the Akindgi and Janissaries left behind, reformed and attacked the French in their rear. All gallantry was unavailing—they were almost all killed or taken. The German knights fell around their sacred banners. The day was lost; of the ten thousand prisoners taken, nearly all were massacred on the following day by Bajazet, who sat out from dawn till evening watching, according to the custom of his race, the gratifying spectacle of slaughter.

This dashed the hopes of the Greek Christians, and they began to prepare for the last hours of their Imperial City. But Bajazet was called away to his Eastern Asiatic frontier, where the Mongols were making fierce inroads on his territory, under their famous leader Tamerlane. A respite was thus granted while thus occupied, for the army of Bajazet was annihilated at Angora, and he himself was slain. No doubt the news of Bajazet's defeat and death was welcome to those who took their walks on the Atrium,

The Walls of Constantinople

no doubt many a good bargain was concluded then and there in a friendly way, when the news from Asia promised better security, and at least a postponement of the Eastern terror. And indeed the Ottoman power was prostrate for awhile after the Battle of Angora, and to make matters worse the sons of Bajazet quarrelled about the succession. In the chaos that ensued even the Greek Empire profited directly, for several portions of lost property were recovered, and no doubt hopes ran high that a turning-point in its fortunes had arrived, that the dark clouds of Eastern predominance so long threatening were to be finally dispelled, and that the sun of Rome would shine again over Byzantium.

But the old terror revived again, though not perhaps to the same extent. Certainly, ere long the Turks were knocking at the city gates again. This time under Musa, a son of Bajazet, who on being released from captivity in Tamerlane's tents, joined in the fray of brothers, and laid siege to Constantinople, because the emperor supported the claims of the eldest brother Solyman, who had taken unto himself the Sultanate of his father's European possession, but had been overcome and slain by Mahomed the younger son.

Manuel II Palæologus, Greek emperor, besought

Seraglio Point

the protection of Mahomed, and for a time a Turkish army actually garrisoned the Castle of Cæsar. But Mahomed had to take his troops back to Asia. There he overcame and slew his brother Musa, and then, all rival claimants having been removed, became Sultan of his father's dominions.

But a few years longer was the respite granted to the failing power of Byzantium. John VII Palæologus retained some semblance of Imperial dignity; but under his successor, a bearer of Constantine's illustrious name, the death-knell sounded alike to the house of Palæologus and to the Roman Empire of the East. The curtain rang down on what may be called the second act of the drama of Byzantium—the reign of the Christian emperors. The curtain rose again on a scene strewn with ruins of Imperial splendour, on heaps of slain, the victims of the conqueror's lust of blood, and the succession of emperors in the Imperial City of the East was restored by one of the greatest and perhaps the most cruel of the able sons of Othman.

Mahomed II the Conqueror broke the proud record of those stout walls of Constantinople, and made the place his own. The ancient capital of the Ottomans, Broussa, and the more recent one, Adrianople, receded into the background; the former to become a relic of

The Walls of Constantinople

satisfied ambitions, treated with the respect usually meted out to a stepping-stone, the latter a mere base for frontier defence. Mahomed transformed all the life of his nation, and centred it in the City of Constantine, choosing that part of it where Byzas first landed, the point of the promontory. For here he separated a space of eight furlongs from the point to the triangle and built his Seraglio.

And here the history of Constantinople continued its course with just that break of a few days when ownership was forcibly transferred. Nor did the religious life of the city suffer any lengthy interruption. True, the monasteries disappeared, the Cross fell from the Christian churches, the Crescent added minarets, and due ceremony made them into mosques. But who can say that the religious life had ceased with the alteration in creed and dogma. And the Turks with some exceptions, usually political, have always respected the faith of others.

It must have been one of the most marvellous and astounding scenes ever witnessed by mortal eyes that took place not long after the city fell, and long before the sights and signs of the desolation there wrought had been removed. The Greek remnant had gathered together and returned in crowds as soon as they had sufficiently been assured of their lives, their liberties,

Seraglio Point

and the free exercise of their religion. To solemnize this fast the Sultan held an investiture on old Byzantium lines, with all the pomp and traditional splendour of the ceremony, an investiture of the Patriarch of Greek Orthodoxy. With his own hand the Conqueror delivered into the hands of Gennodius the crosier or pastoral staff, the symbol of his ecclesiastical office. His Holiness was then conducted to the Gate of the Seraglio, presented with a horse richly caparisoned, and led by viziers and pashas to the palace allotted for his residence.

And this happened within the Seraglio walls! Surely an astounding event. The successor to the throne and empire of the Cæsars, the conqueror whose hands were red with the blood of massacred Christians, the victorious leader of that fanatic race whose life is more influenced by their creed than that of perhaps any other human community, himself approved the chosen Patriarch, the head of his new subjects' religion, and with his own hands elevated him to that high office. Thus from the centre of Constantine's city in its new aspect of purely oriental colouring, the Seraglio, the latticed prison of those whose privilege it is to give birth to the sons of Islam, new life was given to Greek Orthodoxy by him whose sword had hitherto been raised against it.

The Walls of Constantinople

So the life of the old city, the heart of a new empire continued, and one ruler followed another, and like those of the second act, some were good, others bad, but none wholly indifferent. Another Bajazet followed on Mahomed the Conqueror and carried on the victorious traditions of his house. Mahomed died suddenly among his soldiers, leaving two sons, who contested for the sovereignty, as has so often happened in the history of empires raised by the hand of one strong man. Zizimes, the younger son, suggested a division of the empire, Bajazet to rule over Roumelia, Zizimes to govern Anatolia with the Hellespont as boundary between their realms. But Bajazet would none of it. "The Empire is a bride whose favours cannot be shared," he said, and Zizimes was defeated and had to seek refuge at the Courts of other rulers, some Christian, but none of them favourable to the furtherance of his hopes. His death was caused by poison, administered by a servant of the Pope, Alexander Borgia, who thereby gained a reward of 300,000 ducats from the brother Bajazet, the sum that Borgia had agreed to for the deed, and would probably have earned himself had not Charles VIII of France invaded Italy and carried off Zizimes from the guardianship of the Roman Pontiff.

And the romantic history of this chosen spot of

Seraglio Point

Byzas continues within the walls of the Seraglio, one Sultan following another and making his throne secure by murdering others that stood near it. Thus did Selim I to his brethren. He was the youngest, the ablest and most daring of the sons of Bajazet, and in his father's lifetime intrigued against him for possession of the throne. His efforts proved successful. A rabble of soldiers and citizens surrounded the Seraglio and demanded audience of the Sultan. "What is your desire?" inquired Bajazet. "Our Padishah is old and sickly, and we will that Selim shall be our Sultan." So Bajazet abdicated, to die a few days afterwards, and Selim reigned in his stead.

Having secured the throne Selim bent his mind on conquest and the suppression of schism among the followers of the Prophets. The Shiites repudiated the claim to the caliphate of Mahomed's immediate successors, Abu-Dekr, Omar and Othman. So for reasons probably as much political as religious, Selim proclaimed himself champion of Orthodoxy, and sullied his reign by the St. Bartholomew of Ottoman history. In all there were 70,000 of his subjects who held to the Shii doctrine within the Ottoman dominion in Europe and Asia, 40,000 of these were massacred and 30,000 sentenced to perpetual imprisonment. And Selim became Caliph of the Moslem faith.

The Walls of Constantinople

Then follows one whose name looms large in history, Solyman I the Great, his title nobly earned not only by valour in the field, but by wisdom in the council—and he was great among a galaxy of great Christian sovereigns, Charles V, Francis I, Henry VIII and Pope Leo X. The world was then entering on modern times, and many changes were in progress. But who will deny to this the first inception of the modern spirit, the glamour of Romance. The art and practice of war was undergoing a change, the arts of peace were reviving. Holbein was making illustrious sovereigns yet more illustrious by his cunning hand, and the bold spirits of a new Europe found yet newer countries across the seas.

The name of Solyman conjures up visions of the glowing glory of the Eastern Empire, of the force and vigour of Islam, for Selim had enjoined upon his son to carry war into the countries that professed the faith of the Cross. Through this monarch's enterprise was Romance enriched by the story of his wars, as when against Hungary he penetrated even as far as Vienna, which he besieged, what time the Poles came stoutly to the help of Europe, to be rewarded later in history by the partition of Poland and a period of oppression which is not yet ended. With him we connect another glorious name, who brought to his master, victorious

Seraglio Point

on land, new laurels won at sea, Barbarossa, Solyman's great admiral.

Yet another name that rings out from within the walls of the Seraglio, and is known by all who love Romance, is that of Roxalana. Solyman's favourite Sultana in the earlier part of his reign had been a beautiful Circassian. Her son Mustapha inherited his mother's beauty, and was a pattern of manly and chivalrous excellence.

But the Circassian Sultana lost the Imperial favour. A lovely Russian girl, Khourrem ("The joyous one"), enkindled anew the passion of love in the Sultan's breast. She was a slave, she obtained her freedom from her royal lover and induced him to wed her. Khourrem, or as the Christians called her "Roxalana" became Sultana. Her aims and ambition was to forward the chances of her own children, and to that end Mustapha had to be removed. She ruled Solyman to the day of her death, and had the satisfaction of bringing about the murder of Mustapha before she died. He was appointed Governor of Carmania, and so skilfully did Roxalana work upon Solyman that he was at last induced to believe that Mustapha was plotting to usurp the throne. Mustapha was ordered to enter the Sultan's presence alone, and Solyman looking on from an inner chamber saw seven mute executioners carry out his command to strangle his son with the bowstring.

And so the Romance that sheds a glamour over the history enacted within the Seraglio walls flows on, while fortune favours those who merit it, and wrongdoing is often punished by those drastic measures to which these grey embattlements had long become accustomed. Roxalana herself was buried in all due state not a stone's throw from the spot where her sovereign lord afterwards found his rest. But in the two chambers where they lie you will notice a difference. To enter that of Solyman you must take off your shoes, the place is holy ground—the grave of a warrior who is almost a saint. You may, however, pass to the chamber of the "Joyous one" shod as you are. She has no soul, that makes all the difference.

They tell of Selim, Solyman's successor, Roxalana's son, who broke the Law of the Prophet and died drunk; Othman II, of the revolt of the Janissaries and their choice of Sultan—until the seat of Government was moved from the place where Byzas first made his choice and Constantine and his successors reigned, until they in due time gave way to those of the house of Ottoman.

But is the present state of this Seraglio less romantic than in those days of fierce passion un-

Seraglio Point

trammelled and only expressed in blood? The head priest, the Sheik-ul-Islam, has decreed that there is no infringement of the Laws of Islam in its sons expressing higher thoughts by means artistic. And so the life of the Seraglio goes on, peaceful, more beautiful, and just as much Romance as heretofore.

CHAPTER IV

SERAGLIO POINT (*continued*)

SERAGLIO POINT itself, or rather the extreme end of it at least, is now open to the sea. It was not always so, and is only safe now that long-range guns have completely revolutionized the methods of defence.

Where our travellers alighted was a wall flanked by strong towers, 188 in all, says Bondelmontius; this extended all along the coast by the Sea of Marmora, until it joined the angle where the land-walls that cut right across the peninsula commence. Remains, and fine remains, of their sea-wall are still here, at one place dipping their stout foundations into the sea, at others further inland on spots which were in former times the harbour.

No doubt the first wall here was built by Byzas, but it has vanished and made room for the ramparts which Constantine the Great erected to defend his new capital. What yet remains is full of interest and has a beauty of its own.

When looking towards the city from Modar or

Seraglio Point

Kadikeui on the Asiatic side, the city seems to arise from out a girdle of embattled walls, to lose itself in a forest of slender minarets. On approaching these walls their interest increases, for here are arches built up and strange inscriptions, gateways that each contribute many pages to history. Theodosius II and his præfect Constantius have here left records of their rule; the Emperor Theophilus is mentioned in the same manner as the restorer of the walls, and so is the share that Emperor Isaac Angelus contributed to their repair.

No doubt there was much need of walls to guard the ever-extending sea-front of the city along the shore of the Sea of Marmora; for though the Greeks, and after them the Turks, were generally able to forestall an attack by striking first, this policy in the degenerate times of the Empire was not always practicable.

Still the sea-walls were not exposed to the assaults of an enemy to such an extent as were the landward ones; their worst enemy was the sea in its destructive phases, and other elements aided in rendering insecure man's tenure of this precious slip of land.

The traveller must remember the first sight of Constantine's glorious city; he approached it at high noon and saw it melting in a golden haze rising out of tranquil waters, which mirrored faithfully the colour of

The Walls of Constantinople

the sky, while many other colours flamed and fleeted like sparkling diamonds. Yet as we approached Seraglio Point the strength of the current became evident, the current against which those heavy-built sailing craft, aided by their oars, battled so manfully, while it bore other small craft swiftly out into the Sea of Marmora. This current with its constant wear and tear put a severe strain on the foundations of the seaward walls upon Seraglio Point. The traveller's first view was in the fairest of fair weather; but in the winter, when the piercing icy gale tears down through the narrow channel of the Bosphorus, ploughing up its waters to dash them against the facings of the promontory, another side of the picture is revealed, and helps to account for the constant repairs that were needed to keep the seaward ramparts in a proper state of defence. Not only those storms that scourge the racing billows to the charge, but other forces have helped to frustrate man's efforts to shelter himself from fierce foemen and fiercer elements.

For in 447 an earthquake visited this fair spot and wreaked much havoc among the stout walls and stouter towers that Constantine constructed. Again, some three centuries later, a most severe winter held all that Eastern neighbourhood in an iron grip. According to Theophanes, the Black Sea along the northern and

Seraglio Point

western shores was frozen to a distance of one hundred miles from land, and that to a depth of sixty feet. Upon this foundation a huge mass of snow some forty-five feet in height had gathered. With the softer breath of spring the ice broke up, and floating on the swift currents of the Bosphorus came the floes in such numbers that they blocked up the narrower passages and formed a floating barricade across the channel from Scutari to Galata. When this mass in its turn was loosened and drifted south, huge icebergs crashed against the bulwarks, so high that they overtopped the towers and ramparts of the sea-wall, so great that their weight and impetus crushed all that opposed their progress. And thus the walls along the apex of the promontory had to be entirely reconstructed by Michael II, who commenced the work, and his son Theophilus, who completed it.

Author and Artist have discussed most seriously how best to show the traveller these walls along the Sea of Marmora, for there is much to be seen. The Artist loves the view from across the Sea of Marmora seen at sunrise, of the city swimming in a sea of pearly grey; or at sunset, purple against a glowing mass of orange, red and green, colours which are all truthfully reflected in the placid waters. And the centre of the composition is the Seraglio lighthouse. Close behind it

The Walls of Constantinople

rise battlemented walls and towers, and then in tiers of little red roofs above the grey wooden houses, among trees of all kinds, while everywhere the immortal cypress strives after the minarets that stand as sentinels to the many mosques which crown the heights of the city.

Here, too, on that tranquil sheet of water, pages of history have been unrolled, filled up, and set aside for the guidance of future generations. For though the seaward walls were strong and bravely manned, though they were further guarded by a current which could dash an enemy's fleet to atoms on the strong surface of the defences, or carry it harmless out to sea again, many a shipload of adventurous spirits has tried conclusions with the men who held them and the elements which guarded the approaches with equal jealousy.

Perhaps the first serious attempt upon the seaward walls was made by those scourges of the Mediterranean, the Saracens. It was on this occasion that mention is first made of the use of a chain to close the entrance of a harbour against an enemy. It was stretched across the Golden Horn, from a tower near the apex of the promontory to one upon the northern bank.

Those were stirring times, when the sons of Arabia Felix, the first disciples of the Prophet, spread out over

Seraglio Point

all the Mediterranean and the neighbouring countries. They conquered in breathless advance Egypt and all north of Africa, and held their own still in its most western region. They invaded Persia, they overflowed into Spain, overthrew the Gothic monarchy, and remained, despite the heroic efforts of Charlemagne and his Paladins. Syria and the Holy Places were theirs, and they snatched what was best and most worth having among the islands of the Mediterranean. What wonder, then, that they turned their eager, flashing eyes towards Constantinople? As we stand gazing at the beautiful city that rises proudly out of a tranquil sea, the waters become troubled, and dark-blue and iron-grey storm-clouds gather in the south. They race up from the Dardanelles, and hundreds of rakish-looking craft, rigged as those that the traveller may see any day off the north coast of Africa, fly before the wind. The rain falls in torrents, and then suddenly all is still again, the sea is quiet, and the rearguard of the tempest sweeps away up the Bosphorus, to leave the sun in possession of its former battlefield. Even so came the invincible navies of Egypt and Syria, carrying the swarthy sons of Arabia towards the treasures they descried within the walls of Constantine's Imperial City. And up it comes, this storm-cloud, over a smooth sea, and borne on a gentle

The Walls of Constantinople

breeze like a moving forest overshadowing the surface of the strait. Others of their fierce race and fiercer faith were arrayed before the land-walls; and no one of the invaders doubted that any bulwarks, however strong, however well defended, could resist the tide of passionate bravery that was about to break over the devoted city.

But the time was not yet come. Leo III the Isaurian, a man risen from the people to the Imperial Purple through his ability and valour, knew how to defend his own. He had the chain that guarded the entrance to the harbour lowered, and, while the enemy hesitated as to which course to adopt, Greek fireships sailed amongst them carrying destruction as to the Armada. This, and the tempests that arose, so seriously damaged the hitherto invincible fleet that only a few galleys were spared to return to Alexandria and to relate the tale of their moving misadventures.

Though peace was never the lot of the Eastern Empire for any protracted period, it was more than a century later that an unfriendly keel furrowed the waters of the Sea of Marmora. And this time the trouble came from within. Michael II the Stammerer had gained the throne when Leo V the Armenian was slain at the foot of the altar grasping a weighty cross in his hand. Thomas contested Michael's claim

Seraglio Point

and sailed towards the city to enforce his own, but a storm arose and compelled him to withdraw. So Thomas and his galleys are wafted from the scene to be followed shortly afterwards by other hardier adventurers. They came down from the Black Sea, a black cloud their canopy, on black waters that turned to silver where the prows of their vessels cleared a path. Fierce, reckless foes these, who in 865 first made acquaintance with the Eastern Gate of Europe, a goal that for ten centuries represented the sum of their ambition. Fair men of big stature with high cheekbones, speaking a barbarous language, they sped down on the wings of a fierce gale towards the Golden Horn. But here the tempest gained the mastery, and this the first Russian fleet to disturb the peace of Constantinople perished in the storm.

Again a visionary host crowds the further banks with their glittering arms and pennants waving overhead; all the chivalry of the West is here assembled. Their numbers are so great that the Byzantine agents gave up the task of counting them. They came from all the West: from Rome to Britain, from Poland and Bohemia and all Germany under the banner of Conrad the Kaiser. Louis of France too, and his nobles, swelled this throng, who, with the cross emblazoned on their shields and embroidered on their

The Walls of Constantinople

garments, set out upon this conquest of the Holy Land. We see them cross the waters, while hope beats high in their unconquered hearts, and would rather draw a veil over the return of the mere remnant of survivors.

Then later on came others in larger vessels, from the South: Genoese, experienced travellers and determined fighters; also Venetians, the only race of sea-dogs that ever succeeded in an attempt on these sea-walls. A striking scene this. In double line the ships and lighter galleys of the Venetians bore down upon the walls. Soldiers leapt from the swifter sailing craft on to shore and planted scaling-ladders against the walls. In the meantime the heavier ships filled up the gaps with their high poop-decks and turrets, as platforms for those military engines then in use, and from them drawbridges were lowered to the summit of the wall. On the prow of his galley stood Dandolo, the venerable Doge, in full armour. He was the first warrior on the shore. The standard of St. Mark waved from the ramparts and twenty-five of the towers were speedily occupied, the Greeks being driven by fire from the adjacent quarters. But Dandolo decided to forego the advantage thus gained in order to hasten to the aid of his Latin comrades, whose small and exhausted bands were in sore straits among the

Seraglio Point

superior numbers of the Greeks. Nevertheless, their firm aspect awed the coward Emperor Alexius. But he collected a treasure of 10,000 pounds of gold, and basely deserting his wife and people crept into a barque and stole through the Bosphorus and sought safety in an obscure Thracian harbour.

Two mighty heroes of history and Romance, both known as Barbarossa, add yet more colour to the vivid pageant that plays over these placid waters. For further to the south, where the Sea of Marmora narrows into the Channel of the Dardanelles, the Redbeard Frederick, Conrad's son and successor to the throne of the Holy Roman Empire, if not the greatest, at least the best known in the romantic story of the house of Hohenstauffen, crossed into Asia to find, after many deeds of derring do, his watery grave in a small Cilician torrent. There were many who believed he was not dead, but only slumbering deep among the ruins of Kyffhausen—his long red beard grown through the table on which his hand supports his head, the while he dreams even as he has dreamt through all the troublous times that visited Germany. Dreamt while the last scion of his house perished; dreamt while a war of thirty years, provoked like all the cruelest wars by religious differences, devastated the fair fields of Germany and laid waste many a walled city; dreamt while the march of the first Napoleon's armies made Europe tremble—only to awake when all Germany arose and marched towards the Rhine and into the Empire of the third Napoleon, and returning thence to build up a new and stronger empire.

The next to bear the epithet of Barbarossa lived his eventful life when Francis I was King of France and Charles V King of Spain, Naples and the Netherlands, and by election German Emperor, ruled over many states and provinces of the old world and the new.

Solyman I the Great was Sultan and Chief, and reigned at Constantinople, extending the empire of the Crescent by land far into Western Europe, while Barbarossa carried the victorious symbol everywhere in the Mediterranean Sea. His name was Khairedden Pasha, one of four brothers who were trained to merchandise with its usual concomitant piracy, and amassed great wealth in these pursuits. Barbarossa and his brother Urudsh sailed at first under the flag of the Tunisian Sultan but paid tribute to Solyman, and eventually transferred to him their allegiance. They conquered Temnes, Algiers, and all the Barbary coast, which they held as fief of the Porte. All his ventures seemed to be successful. A strong fleet was sent against him under command of Genoa's great admiral,

Seraglio Point

Doria, by Charles V, but Barbarossa defied him. A stately pageant passed down the Sea of Marmora in 1534. Barbarossa and his fleet of eighty-four vessels, with which he scoured the Mediterranean Sea, ravaged the coasts of Italy, Minorca and Spain, and beat the combined fleets of the Emperor, the Pope, and Venice off Prevosa. After many years of successful marauding we see the Turkish fleet return, still under command of their veteran admiral, Barbarossa, whose beard was turning white. A peaceful end in Constantinople was his, and now the body that held that turbulent spirit rests worthily enshrined by the shore of the Bosphorus.

With the passing of Barbarossa a new power first makes its appearance under the walls of old Byzantium, its colours the white ensign emblazoned with St. George's blood-red cross. Tight-built English ships, some of which may possibly have borne their brave part in the defeat of Spain's great Armada, are next seen sailing smoothly upon the waters of the inland sea. They bring messages from Elizabeth, Queen of England, to Amurath II, Sultan and Chief.

Again, a century later, when Ibrahim, an evil ruler, reigned over the Turkish Empire, and excesses of all kinds went unpunished, some English ships lying in the Bosphorus were plundered. It was the custom

The Walls of Constantinople

then in Turkey, when any one had received an injury from a minister or official, for him to put fire on his head and run to the palace. Stout Sir Thomas Bentinck, the English Ambassador—redress for the outrage to English ships having been refused—brought them up from Galata and anchored them immediately before the windows of the Imperial Palace. Adapting the custom we have mentioned, he lighted fires on every yard-arm. No sooner was this seen on shore than the Vizier hastened to the Ambassador, paid him a large sum of money, and engaging to pay the surplus of the sum demanded, besought him to extinguish the warning blaze.

But now, at the bidding of the Author, we move landwards again. As we approach, bearing somewhat to the south of the Seraglio lighthouse, the buildings above us stand out more clearly. Constantine's Church, now Mosque of St. Sophia, looms over all the attendant minarets, relieving the imposing mass of masonry of its too heavy aspect. Near by the Mosque of St. Irene, also of Constantine's building. In this mosque is still kept the chain that barred the Golden Horn to the Turks during the last siege. A long yellow building stands out near St. Sophia, and shows a pillared front to the smooth waters of the Marmora. This is now the Turkish Parliament, though in a short

Seraglio Point

time that young and vigorous assembly is to transfer its deliberations to one of the more gorgeous palaces of the Bosphorus. Fittingly enough it stands almost on the site of the Senate of Roman, Grecian and Byzantine empire. Here centred much of the life of the old City of Constantine, hard by is the Hippodrome which that emperor laid out. It was here that the city's pleasure-seeking denizens met to enjoy the games, the chariot-races, and other pastimes peculiar to that age. What fortunes must have been wagered or dissipated by a single crashing blow of the cæstus, or by one slip of the runner as he left the starting-line! How many a delicate girl must have held her hands in horror to her eyes, when under the brazen tripod fell the charioteer who had swerved too closely to the corner, and drawn down the other competitors with him in his ruin. Here, also, in later times of trouble or internal strife the citizens would meet and clamour to be taken to the palace, there to acclaim a heroic emperor, or abuse an unpopular leader. How fickle and ill-balanced that turbulent cosmopolitan crowd must have been, we realize from the curious history of Justinian.

Justinian, bearing the name of a triumphant law-giver, entered into the heritage of the Roman world in 685. He was a lad of strong passions and feeble intellect. He ruled with a cruelty gross even for that age and place, through the hands of his favourite ministers, a eunuch and a monk, by whose aid he succeeded for ten years in braving the growing hatred of his subjects. A sudden freak, rather than any sense of the justice he habitually outraged, induced the emperor to liberate Leontius, a general of high repute, who, with some of the city's noblest and most deserving men, had suffered imprisonment for above three years. Leontius was promoted to be Governor of Greece. A successful conspiracy was headed by him, the prisons were forced open, and an excited populace swarmed to the Church of St. Sophia, where the Patriarch, taking as text for his sermon, "This is the day of the Lord," influenced the passions of the multitude. They crowded into the Hippodrome, Justinian was dragged before the insurgent judges, who clamoured for his immediate death. But Leontius, already clothed in the Purple, was merciful, and spared the life of his benefactor's son, the scion of so many emperors, and, slightly mutilated about the face, the deposed sovereign was banished to the Crimea. Here he abode, and watched events of which the news trickled through but sparingly. News of another revolution arrived, in which Leontius fell from power a mutilated victim, to make room for Apsimar, who

Seraglio Point

henceforth called himself Tiberius. Meanwhile Justinian had contracted an alliance with the Khan of the Chazars by marrying that chief's sister, Theodora. But the Khan proved venal, and bribed by the gold of Constantinople sought to bring about Justinian's death. In vain, for Theodora's conjugal love frustrated this design, and Justinian with his own hands strangled the two emissaries of the Khan. He then sent Theodora back to her brother. Thereupon Justinian sailed away, and with the aid of the Bulgarians laid siege to his own city, which having tired of their present ruler admitted him to the throne again.

So we find Justinian in the Hippodrome surrounded by his people. The two usurpers, Leontius and Apsimar, were dragged one from his prison, the other from his palace, and cast prostrate and in fetters before the throne, where Justinian sat and watched the chariot-race, a foot on the neck of each vanquished rival. The fickle people meanwhile shouted in the words of the psalmist, "Thou shalt trample on the asp and basilisk, and on the lion and the dragon shalt thou set thy foot." Even in those early days the use of a well-known text, taken conveniently apart from its context, was a political weapon not to be despised.

When the games were over Leontius and Apsimar were taken down to the Kynegion, the place of

The Walls of Constantinople

execution near the Church of St. George of Mangana, and there Justinian requited the ill-judged clemency of his former conqueror. But his own capricious cruelty so disgusted the troops he had dispatched to carry out the sentence of those on whom the Emperor had sworn to be avenged, that they revolted, and invested Bardanes with the Imperial Purple. Destitute of friends, and deserted by his Barbarian guard, there was none to ward off the stroke of the assassin, and by it Justinian, along with his innocent son, Tiberius, perished, and thus ended the line of Heraclius.

THE PALACE OF HORMISDAS OR JUSTINIAN.

This place is full of the memories of dark and strange events, it is the Palace of Justinian.

CHAPTER V

THE WALLS BY THE SEA OF MARMORA

Let us go ashore under the sea-walls of Constantinople. We now approach the white Seraglio lighthouse, keeping a little south of it and yet a little more, rounding a slight bend of the coast to westward. Here, beyond a strong square tower which formerly showed a flare of Grecian fire to guide the mariner, is a stretch of beach, Author and Artist insist on landing. The tower we left on our right joins on to a large front of masonry, built stoutly of rough stones as you may see where the walls are broken, and where a few marble pillars frame hollow openings for the windows. This place is full of the memories of dark and strange events, it is the Palace of Justinian.

Old chroniclers called this the Palace of Hormisdas, or Hormouz, Prince of Persia, who sought refuge here with Constantine the Great. Others, again, suggest that this palace was built by Justinian himself before he began his long and useful reign.

At any rate, great and famous names occur to us

The Walls of Constantinople

as we survey these ruins. It is an astounding chapter of history this, which tells how Justinian came to inherit the Imperial Purple. His uncle Justin was the founder of his house, a simple Dacian peasant who left his native village and the flocks he tended to enter the military service of the Eastern Empire. Through his own strength, his own ability and valour in the field, Justin the Dacian peasant rose step by step until he took his place next to Cæsar himself in importance. Then when the Emperor Anastasius died, after carefully excluding his own kinsman from the throne, Justin was acclaimed Emperor by the unanimous consent of those who knew him to be brave and gentle, his soldiers, and by those who held him to be orthodox, the priests. So in his old age, for he was sixty-eight when Anastasius died, Justin climbed the throne and reigned for nine years. Strange, too, it is, that he and yet another ruler of his time, Theodoric, the King of Italy, even in those days when learning was by no means uncommon, should both have been unable to read and write. Justin had brought his nephew Justinian out of Dacia, and had him educated in Constantinople to be trained for the Purple.

His was a curious and eventful reign. Of great strength and comely of face, full of the best intentions and restless in his pursuit of knowledge, Justinian

The Walls by the Sea of Marmora

entered into his inheritance; he had been his uncle Justin's right hand, and so was well acquainted with all the devious ways of statecraft. So everything promised well, and in a measure he succeeded. The wars he undertook were brought to a successful issue, the laws he framed should have earned him the people's gratitude, yet Justinian was not beloved.

No doubt these walls could tell the reason—you may almost hear them whisper, " Theodora, the actress, the dancer, and Justinian's empress." Surely those were stirring times, when Justinian and Theodora sat side by side upon the throne, when circus and streets rang with the cries of factions, Blue and Green. And Theodora favoured Blue—her cause for doing so dates back to the day of her earliest appearance in Constantinople—in the theatre. Here she and her sisters, daughters of Acacius, whose office was to tend the wild beasts that the Green faction kept for the games, were brought by their mother in the garb of suppliants. The Green faction received them with contempt, the Blues with compassion, and hence the reason that Theodora favoured that colour.

Then some time elapsed, during which it were best not to follow Theodora's fortunes. During this epoch a son was born to her. Years after, the father of the child when dying told him: " Your mother is an

The Walls of Constantinople

empress." The son of Theodora hastened to Constantinople, hurried to the palace to present himself —and was never seen again. When in seclusion at Alexandria Theodora had a vision which told her that one day she would wear the Purple, so she returned to Constantinople, and ere long won Justinian's love. So they reigned side by side, and Justinian first of that name is still called "the Great." Let whatever evil she may have done be forgotten. Are not the scandals of that time softened by the mists of romance which enshroud them, for all but those who like to peer about among the secrets of dead men, and to cavil at their failings, and tear what tatters of reputation they can find into yet smaller shreds.

Nearly four centuries had passed, and yet again the Palace of Justinian was witness of imperial weakness. The Greek fleet rode at anchor beneath the windows of the palace, and from his ship the Admiral Romanus Lecapenus made his way into the presence of the Emperor. There he demanded of Constantine VII, called Porphyrogenitus, a share in the government of the Empire, and was proclaimed co-Emperor. At one time during this reign five Cæsars wore the Purple; he who was born in it, Constantine VII, Porphyrogenitus, ranked least among them, but he survived them all in office to die of poison, it is said

The Walls by the Sea of Marmora

administered by Theophane, the wife of his son, Romanus II.

Again a woman plays a strong part in the history of these palace walls. A woman of low origin, this wife of the Eastern Emperor, son of Constantine VII, and under the careless reign of her good-natured husband, she made her vigorous personality a power in the land. Four years did Romanus II reign, and in that time did nothing that could afford the historian excuse for lingering on his name. Strongly built and fair to look upon, his time was spent in the pleasures he best loved. While the two brothers Leo and Nicephones triumphed over the Saracens, the Emperor's days were spent in strenuous leisure. He visited the circus in the morning, feasted the senators at noon, and then adjourned to the sphæristerium, the tennis-court, where he achieved his only victories. From time to time he would cross over to the Asiatic side, and there hunt the wild boar, returning to the palace well content with what he probably considered a good day's work.

Theophane tired of her useless spouse, and mingled for him the same deadly draught which killed his father. She then aspired to reign in the name of her two sons, Basil and Constantine, one five, the other only two years old, but found she could not support the

The Walls of Constantinople

weight of such responsibility, and looked about for some one to protect her.

She found the man in Nicephorus Phocas, who was then accounted the bravest soldier in the land. In other ways he appeared suitable, for he combined with the military genius that had led to many victories the reputation of a saint. For the rest, in person he was deformed, so that perchance Theophane's spacious heart was aided by her head when she set about to choose the successor to Romanus in her affections. Another like him lived many centuries later and ruled over England, Richard of Gloucester—and through the hazy veil wherewith romance so kindly clothes the crude outlines of history, it is difficult to decide to what extent the religious practices and utterances of these two monarchs were prompted by sincerity or guile. For Nicephorus wore hair-cloth, fasted, and clothed his conversation with pious terms; he even wished to retire from the business of this world into the serene seclusion of a monastery. Whatever the value of the sentiments he expressed, the people and the Patriarch trusted him, and so he was invested with the command of the oriental armies.

No sooner had he received the leaders and the troops than he marched boldly into Constantinople at their head. He trampled on his enemies, avowed his

The Walls by the Sea of Marmora

correspondence with the Empress, and assumed the title of Augustus. Unlike his double, Richard, he spared the lives of the young princes.

After some dubious dealings, the silence of the clergy made his union with Theophane possible, so he reached the height of his ambition—the Imperial Purple. But, strange to say, the once so popular general when in the Purple lost the affection of his people. No doubt the faults were equally divided, the Greeks disliked him for his parsimony, and he had ample precedent of how easily a fickle population can change from favour to fierce hatred. A demonstration of this change caused Nicephorus to fortify the Palace of Justinian; he had been stoned by his own people, and had barely reached the palace in safety.

Whilst standing by the sea under this mass of ruins, let us go back to a winter's night in 969. The additions to the palace that Nicephorus had made to guard him against the fury of his subjects had that day been completed. The gates were locked and bolted, the windows strongly barred, and, as a further precaution, the Emperor had moved from the couch and room he generally occupied at night, and lay asleep stretched on a bear-skin on the floor of a smaller chamber. But treachery lurked within the palace walls; murderous plans were rife, and they were conceived in the brain of an adulterous empress. And listening by those dark waves we hear the sound of muffled oars. A boat takes shape in the gloom at the foot of the palace stairs. Headed by John Zimisces, lover of Theophane, a man of small stature but great strength and beauty, and a soldier of renown, shadowy forms ascend a rope ladder, lowered from a window by some female attendants. Other conspirators were hidden in Theophane's most private chambers; they reached the Emperor's retreat, and with much cruelty and insult Nicephorus II Phocas was done to death.

John Zimisces reigned in his stead, but ere he was allowed to assume full power with the sanction of the Church he had to face at least one upright man. On the threshold of St. Sophia, whither he went to his coronation, the intrepid Patriarch stopped his progress, charged him with entering the Holy Place with blood upon his hands, and demanded, as a sign of penance, he should separate himself from his guilty companion.

So Theophane was banished from the place that still is haunted by her baleful influence, and died unmourned in exile.

Another vision, less sombre, equally dramatic and more fleeting, comes and fades away. Amaury, king

The Walls by the Sea of Marmora

of Jerusalem, visits Manuel Comunenus in 1170, to implore his aid against Saladin. A brief pathetic scene thus re-enacts itself, brief as the reign of those, the Christian Kings of David's Royal City, pathetic in the waste of life, the misery, the abject hopelessness that marked those chivalrous enterprises known to us as the Crusades.

One final scene before we turn away from this historic spot, the last scene in its history, and splendid in its utter despair. Here, at the last siege of Constantinople by the Turks, stout-hearted Peter Guliano and his gallant catalans held out when all else was lost.

A steep incline leads from the beach, past little wooden houses perched anywhere against the ruined walls. They look like that old house—that dear old house—Hans Andersen speaks of in the shortest of his fairy tales. We climb up the steep ascent, and at the top find more ruins—the base of a gigantic marble pillar, broken arches built of brick and glorious in their subdued colour; and then—the railway. Yes, gentle readers, the Roumelian Railway, to give it its full and awesome title. And we must follow this railway if we would see more of the city walls. You may walk anywhere you like along the single track. A little pathway winds about here and there and everywhere, and on either hand are houses, some of wood, some more pretentious, scattered about with irregularity.

Above us is the ridge on which the Hippodrome, theatre, and circus used to stand in days when a pleasure-loving population spent time and money in much the same way as do some Western nations of this day. No doubt they too considered themselves sportsmen; no doubt they too danced abject attendance and stood numerous dinners to the stalwart hero who was awarded his "Blue" or his "Green," as the case might be. And as to some forms of sport in those days of the Byzantine Empire, we have already given account of one sportsman's strenuous day, the Emperor Romanus, and we have seen how his wife discouraged his proclivities, by methods effective, but far too drastic for the present age.

Ancient chroniclers make mention of a polo-ground, but it is too much to expect such very learned men to tell you how the game was played. Yet this concerns the Author and Artist nearly, for both have spent much time and pleasantly in the saddle. No doubt the game, under whatever rules, was extremely picturesque; the life, the colour, the movement of horses and men engaged in such a keen pursuit can never fail to give a series of brilliant and entrancing pictures. But when

The Walls by the Sea of Marmora

you come to details! No trim pigskin saddles, but possibly some coloured bolsters, with loose bits of braid or tassels for adornment; no doubt bright-coloured brow-bands—that abomination! And then the ball. The Artist wonders whether it was painted the colour of one of the many factions that made up the political life of the city—Blue, Green, or Red—or whether, like keen sportsmen, such differences were dropped in contests of this kind.

Undoubtedly party feeling ran high when races—chariot-races chiefly—were in progress at the Hippodrome. These Green and Blue kept up a continual wordy warfare, and no doubt backed their own fancy colour with the same indiscriminate ardour not altogether unfamiliar even in the world's greatest Empire of to-day. And here again another likeness presents itself, for the games were played and contests entered by men paid to show their skill, while thousands sat and watched, shouted advice, or yelled their disapproval, though quite unable and unwilling to venture on the game themselves.

Of fishing there is no mention as a sport. The Author much regrets to have to make this statement, as he would have liked to give Walton's disciples of to-day some account of how their gentle art was plied in the days of Old Byzantium. But then the necessary

The Walls of Constantinople

implements were not available, for the West had not yet swamped the East with cheap manufactures and easily-twisted pins in penny packets.

The Artist has watched with interest gallant attempts with the bent pin to draw fish from the Bosphorus. The small boy with his little rod so evidently cut by himself, and one sticky little hand full of dead flies, served to remind the Artist of his own efforts in that line. Oh the unholy joy of impaling a fat bluebottle on the point of that bent pin! But the chief pleasure of this form of sport is lacking on the banks of the Bosphorus; the long arm of the law does not interfere, and so the charm of the "strictly forbidden" is denied you.

A noble form of sport was practised in the Middle Ages, and until comparatively recent times a pastime that has given rise to much that is beautiful in poetry and painting—the art of falconry. This was a favourite pursuit of many a sultan, this and hunting with those strong hounds whose descendants (though to judge from their appearance one can scarcely believe it) now roam the streets of Constantinople, and act as rather unsatisfactory scavengers.

A mighty sportsman in these particulars was Achmet I, who reigned in the beginning of the seventeenth century. It was in this monarch's reign that

The Walls by the Sea of Marmora

the Turkish theologians propounded a peculiar doctrine. Achmet had ordered all the dogs in Constantinople to be transported to Scutari, on the opposite side of the Bosphorus, with an allowance of bread and carrion for their maintenance. By a later decree they were again removed, this time to an island sixteen miles away, where they all perished for want of food. The lives of dogs, though held unclean by Turks, were deemed of such importance that the Sultan thought fit to ask the Mufti whether it were lawful to kill them. After due deliberation the head of Islam answered (for he can give no fetvah or decree unless first consulted) that every dog had a soul, and therefore it was not lawful to kill them.

What subsequently happened to the dogs is not recorded; some legends say that they swam back to their old haunts, and incidentally to their ladies, who it appears had not been exiled. Certain it is that their lives were spared, for there are plenty to be seen everywhere in Old Stamboul and its neighbourhood, for of course Achmet, a pious Moslem, would not disregard the Mufti's momentous utterance.

That Achmet was a pious man is without doubt; his mosque bears witness to his devotion, a mosque which far out-rivalled that of St. Sophia in the splendour of its decoration, though it is somewhat smaller.

The Walls of Constantinople

Great treasures were spent upon this mosque, and neither trouble nor expense were spared to make it more glorious than any other. But Achmet left behind an unpaid, discontented army and an empty treasury, having grasped the secret of laying up for himself treasure in heaven by the ingenious method of robbing other people's possessions on earth. In those days East and West drew nearer to each other than heretofore. Where formerly the West had paid sporadic visits which were by no means always welcome, commerce had begun to spread its tendrils, and found the policy of Turkey singularly liberal. So all the greater nations established relations on that friendly basis with the Porte; England, France and Holland had each a regularly accredited ambassador at the Ottoman Court. This inaugurated a more peaceful method of settling disputes, as, for example, when the Moors of Granada brought to the Sultan their grievance against France, telling how, in their passage to that country on being expelled from Spain, they had suffered bodily harm and loss of goods. A chaus or ambassador from Sultan Achmet to Henry IV soon set matters right without resort to what diplomats call the *ultima ratio*. While on the subject of ambassadors a romantic story should be told, an incident which nearly disturbed the peace of Europe.

The Walls by the Sea of Marmora

Achmet left seven sons, all infants, into whose hands he could not place the reins of government, which he himself had held but loosely. On his accession he had not found it necessary to clear his path and prevent further trouble by the usual remedy of fratricide. His only brother, Mustapha, was thoroughly incompetent, almost an idiot. Yet it was he whom Achmet declared as his successor, and the Mufti, the Ulema, the high college of priests, and the high officers of State approved his choice and placed Mustapha on the throne. In all his acts Mustapha emphasized his incapacity to rule, and one of them went near to cause a rupture with France. It fell out thus.

Two captives languished in the dungeons of a castle on the Black Sea. One was Prince Koreski, a Pole, who had been taken prisoner in Moldavia during the last reign, and was confined here because he had refused to turn Mahomedan. The other who shared Koreski's cell was Rigault, a Frenchman, who kept up a clandestine correspondence with a fellow-countryman, Martin, Secretary to the French Embassy at Constantinople. Now Martin loved a young Polish lady, who with her mother and her maid was held prisoner by the Turks. Martin succeeded in purchasing the freedom of these ladies by a payment to the Sultan of two thousand five hundred crowns. But

The Walls of Constantinople

when the ladies returned to their home in Poland the father refused to accede to the arrangement and practically forbade the banns. So in his trouble Martin confided all to his friend Rigault, who in his turn told all to the Prince. Now Koreski was a man of great influence in his own country, and told Rigault to assure his friend that if their escape from prison could be managed, Martin should not pine long for his lady-love.

So Martin set to work right eagerly. A Greek priest who went to visit the prisoners concealed under his garments a long piece of pack-thread, and by these means the captives gained their freedom. Mustapha's police sought diligently, but only managed to discover Martin's share in the transaction, so the whole French Embassy were put under arrest. The ambassador was confined in the Grand Vizier's Palace, Rigault and the domestics were put to the torture.

The protests of the English and Dutch ambassadors failed to move Mustapha, and it was only through large donations to the chief officers of State that the French Embassy was set at liberty.

While listening to the tales the Author has to tell, our travellers have picked their way along the railway-line, and have threaded in and out among the picturesque inhabitants of this quarter. Here

THE SEA WALL.

These remnants of massive walls with battlemented summits, or perhaps little wooden houses are perched on top.

The Walls by the Sea of Marmora

stand broken arches, loopholes looking out to sea; there remnants of massive walls with battlemented summits, or perhaps little wooden houses are perched on top, with their latticed windows; while beneath them one sees gardens, where part of a prophecy is at least fulfilled, for every man has his own fig-tree. And as we walk on these remains, the walls recede inland and disappear altogether, for here was formerly a harbour, and the name of the station we are passing, Koum Kapoussi—sand-gate—was given to the gate that opened out on the harbour of the Kontoscalion. A fair-sized harbour too, now all silted up and built over.

What life and bustle was here in the days of old Byzant, those days of the great traders from the East, West and South. And what stores of treasure were landed at this spot. Work from the looms of Greece was stapled here, manufacturers of linen, woollen and silk—the former industries which had flourished since the days of Homer, the latter introduced about the time of Justinian. Perhaps it was here that those rich gifts arrived for Basil I from his generous friend, Danielis, the rich matron of Peloponnesus, who had adopted him as her own. Doubtless the goods she sent were products of the Grecian looms. Even an Emperor of Byzantium must have greeted

The Walls of Constantinople

with pleased astonishment the beauty of the presents sent by his friend. A carpet large enough to overspread the floor of a new church, woven of fine wool and cunningly designed to represent and rival the brilliant eyes that adorn the peacock's tail. Of silk and linen each six hundred pieces, the latter so exquisitely fine that an entire piece might be rolled into the hollow of a cane, the silk dyed with Tyrian crimson, and the whole ornamented with fair needlework.

Duties were raised on all the goods that entered, and went towards suggesting the splendour of the Emperor and his Court. It is not possible to accurately compute the value of the goods and the vast sums they realized, but at least one traveller of experience was much impressed by what he witnessed here. A Jew, and therefore no mean authority on pecuniary matters, one Benjamin of Tudela, speaks of the riches of Byzantium, which he visited in the twelfth century—

"It is here in the Queen of Cities that the tributes of the Greek Empire are annually deposited, and the lofty towers are filled with precious magazines of silk, purple and gold. It is said that Constantinople pays each day to her sovereign 20,000 pieces of gold, which are levied on the shops, taverns, and markets, on the

The Walls by the Sea of Marmora

merchants of Persia and Egypt, of Russia and Hungary, of Italy and Spain, who frequent the capital by sea and land." Nowadays the main source of public revenue is the crushing import duty on all new articles of 11 per cent., soon with the consent of the powers to be raised to 15. Until recently every Turkish subject resident in the capital paid also a capitation tax in lieu of the military service, which is now to be endured by all alike who cannot pay an exemption fee of £50.

We walk on but a little further along the line, still past ruined walls and towers, and come to yet another gate, Yedi Kapoussi, or New Gate. This was the entrance to a very ancient harbour—the oldest, it is said, along this stretch of coast. Its origin is ascribed to Eleutherius, who was one of the first to see this city rise. The site of the harbour is now entirely covered, and market-gardens are to be seen where formerly war-galleys sought refuge from enemies or elements.

It is not certain at what date this harbour was abandoned, but it had happened before the final assault by Mahomed the Conqueror. The difficulty of keeping this harbour dredged must have been very considerable, for not only does the sea constantly cast sand along this coast, but just here the Lycus,

The Walls of Constantinople

an historic stream, empties its waters into the Sea of Marmora, and deposits at its mouth an ever-increasing burden of rich mud washed down from above.

According to tradition the harbour of Eleutherius served not only for the safety of the Empire's ships of war, but also as an entrance to the slave-market, which is said to have been somewhere in this neighbourhood. It is too sad, sadder than all the tales of cunning intrigue, ferocious crime and unscrupulous ambitions which make up so large a portion of the history enacted behind these city walls, to remember the vast multitude of human beings bartered here like the beasts of the field. Innocent victims of misfortune were sold here, and many families must have met, possibly for the last time on earth, in this ghastly and degrading place, while captives that had escaped the sword in some bloody war of conquest or reprisal were here put up to auction, to be led away by their new masters and die in hopeless misery.

But that sombre vision vanishes too under the sun that draws such brilliant colours from the ruined walls that so long sheltered this chartered and unchallenged iniquity, and we move onward by a laughing sea towards the west, turning south by a point or two as we leave the harbour of Eleutherius behind us.

We linger for a minute at the Gate of Psamathia

The Walls by the Sea of Marmora

—sand-gate again—and look out across the sea from a shady Turkish café standing on a small spit of land that shelters a tiny harbour to westward. Here are a number of those craft that we have seen flying down the Bosphorus under full sail. The leisurely process of unloading is going forward, and stacks of wood are piled up carelessly and anywhere without undue hurry, while nimble-footed donkeys thread their way amongst the merchandise, and the driver follows sunk in his Eastern reverie. And everywhere are dogs lounging together in little knots like elderly gentlemen in a club smoking-room (and always in the way), taking no interest in anything save the adventurous flies, and only giving an occasional languid snap at them.

From here we thread our way through a maze of little narrow lanes of quaint wooden houses teeming with life and colour. Here at a street corner a modest general store, showing some melons in their thick green coats, one with a large slice cut out by way of charity or advertisement, the green skin merging from pale lemon to a delicious crimson. Near these a basketful of ripe tomatoes in their flaring red, contrasting strongly with the golden green of luscious grapes exposed for sale on delicate pink paper; yet all these colours harmonize, and in the cool depths of the

The Walls of Constantinople

background the owner sits and drowses cross-legged, amid all their glory.

As we continue on our way we lose sight of these ancient sea-walls, for we have to turn inland awhile and follow the high-road that leads out into the open country. But now and then we see between the houses a glimpse of high towers and battlements in front of us. We turn down from the high-road, recross the railway-line, and find ourselves again amongst imposing ruins. Standing out boldly is a fine tower, almost intact. As we draw nearer to it we understand how it came by its name, for this is the Marble Tower. It is a building of four storeys, constructed from the topmost string course downwards of large marble blocks, its white and gleaming foundations washed by the blue waters of the Sea of Marmora. To eastward, and joined on to the Tower, stands a two-storied mass of masonry, with deep-arched window looking out to sea. These are the ruins of a castle that stood here to mark the place where sea- and land-walls joined. Most probably it was the residence of some high military officer. Surely a pleasant place to live in, strong and secure, with a spacious courtyard and perhaps a shady garden therein.

Or more likely still, this space, now a market-garden, was the scene of military life for many

THE MARBLE TOWER.

Standing out boldly is a fine tower, almost intact. This is the Marble Tower.

The Walls by the Sea of Marmora

centuries; here the heavy-armed infantry of Roman tradition made way for lighter troops whose dexterity replaced the armour they had abandoned.

What discussions must have taken place when news came that a powder had been invented in the West, a powder which could hurl stones and leaden shot with greater impetus than any engines then in use, that a breast-plate and helmet and even stone walls were no protection against this deadly stuff. And the sentry pacing the ramparts on his lonely post at night would ruminate upon this matter, and wonder what power of evil could let loose a force capable of destroying both the stout walls under him and that fair marble gleaming white in the light of the moon. Probably with the simple faith of his time he laid the whole matter at the door of Satan himself, and his chosen agents—the workers of black magic—and no doubt glanced fearfully out to sea and crossed himself piously when he realized how much influence these unpleasant people still possessed even in a Christian world which caused them to be burned on the barest suspicion of such malpractices.

Moon and stars and the plashing waves are now the only guardians of these walls.

CHAPTER VI

THE GOLDEN GATE

A SMALL, deep-arched postern leads our travellers out of the precincts of the ruins that surround the Marble Tower. The masonry above the postern bears inscriptions dating back to the days when several emperors reigned together. Basil II and Constantine IX, who have been already mentioned in connection with the Palace of Justinian, left records of their reign upon this section of the walls. The postern leads us outside the city walls, and as we turn for a last glance at the Marble Tower and the wonderful view it commands, we notice a strange Byzantine device carved on its keystone.

A narrow tongue of land runs out into the sea just here, and under its lee the cargo of several small sailing craft is being leisurely brought ashore, for staring us in the face is commercial enterprise and all it entails in the shape of a tannery. Here in former days was open country which many a time had witnessed thrilling scenes. For at this small harbour

POSTERN, WITH INSCRIPTIONS OF BASIL II. AND CONSTANTINE IX.

A small, deep-arched postern leads out of the precincts of the ruins that surround the Marble Tower.

The Golden Gate

the hero of a victorious campaign in Asia Minor was wont to land, and with him his troops. Spoils taken in the war were stacked and hapless prisoners paraded to follow in procession through the Golden Gate at the conqueror's chariot wheels. From this harbour the Turkish fleet of 305 vessels attempted to cut off the five gallant ships that brought provisions from the island of Scio to the city during the last siege; these managed to force their way to the Golden Horn.

The sentry on the ramparts over the postern we have left behind us, looking over this rolling plain, would see the glittering domes and pinnacles of yet another lordly place away on the curving sea-coast—the palace of the Hebdomon. This, it appears, served as a rustic retreat for the emperors of the East. Important functions took place there, for here Valens was inaugurated as colleague of his brother, the Emperor Valentine, and proclaimed Augustus. And others followed him, such as Arcadius and Honorius, raised to imperial rank by Theodosius the Great, Leo the Great and Leo the Armenian, and he with whose fate we became familiar when talking of Theophane, Nicephorus II Phocas.

But we will hasten away from that malodorous evidence of progress, the tannery, for we are strongly drawn towards those towering ruins gleaming through

The Walls of Constantinople

the dark cypresses. We cross the railway-line and note where it has cut a path through the ancient defences of Byzantium.

Climbing a bank, we reach a little Turkish cemetery, its weird and tumbling tombstones shaded by those solemn, watchful cypress-trees. Now look towards the walls: between us and them is a deep fosse, where fig-trees grow and throw out their twisted branches as if to protect these ancient ramparts from crumbling further to decay. Ivy in dense dark masses clings to the crenulated scarp, and beyond that a broad roadway, all neglected, rises in gentle gradient till it turns sharply towards an archway, guarded on either hand by massive towers built of blocks of polished marble.

This is the Golden Gate, the "Porta Aurea" of so many glorious moments in the life of Constantine's great city.

Here the procession that had formed on the plain down by the harbour made its triumphal entry, and worthy was this monument in those days to serve as frame to a conquering Augustus. Walls and towers were crowned with parapets, over which glittered the glint of armour and the flashing light of spear-heads. The gates, too, were all on fire with the precious metal from which its name comes, though it now lives

THE GOLDEN GATE, FROM SOUTH-WEST.

This is the Golden Gate, the "Porta Aurea" of so many glorious moments in the life of Constantine's great city.

The Golden Gate

only in memory. Statues and sculptured ornaments added to the splendour of which the only traces now to be seen are some remains of marble cornices, and, at the south-western angle of the northern tower, a Roman eagle with wings outspread in solitary grandeur.

The Golden Gate had three archways, of which the central one was loftier and wider, like those more familiar to us in the Roman Forum. These were dedicated to Severus and Constantine respectively, and the gilded gates of these three arches were those of Mompseueste, placed here by Nicephorus Phocas to commemorate his victorious campaign in Cilicia.

Of all the many works of art that went to decorate the Golden Gate no traces but those just mentioned can be found; but there are records of them, and some are strange reading—for instance, the transactions between an English ambassador to the Porte from 1621–28, Sir Thomas Rowe and the "Great Treasurer." Good Sir Thomas, it appears, had mentioned in his dispatches that two bas-reliefs which figured here were really well worthy of note. This led to another English gentleman, a Mr. Petty, being sent to Constantinople to see to the removal of these treasures to the Earl of Arundel, who sought to share them with the Duke of Buckingham. Much English

The Walls of Constantinople

gold changed hands and found its way into the hungry pockets of the Great Treasurer, who, like all other Turkish high officials before and since, had frequent and pressing need of money, and was not plagued with petty scruples as to the means employed to obtain it. The bargain was completed and all arrangements made, but at the last moment, when it came to removing these marbles, the populace, under the castellan of the castle, rose in mutiny. The precious life of the Great Treasurer was in danger, and as he had probably pouched the money by that time, he discovered it to be quite impossible to carry out his part of the contract, at least for the present; and stout Sir Thomas reported to head-quarters in these words, "So I despair to effect therein your grace's service, and it is true, though I could not get the stones, yet I allmost raised an insurrection in that part of the cytty."

We are standing now before the ruined remains of this, the culminating point of many a page of glorious achievement in the history of the Eastern capital. But let us now regard it with the eye of retrospection; let the past ages envelop the broken, ivy-covered monument and restore it to us in its pristine glory, for we, too, would take part in the splendid pageant that once animated this now-deserted stronghold.

The Golden Gate

So we go back into the depth of time from which perchance we issued. The fourth century of the Christian era is big with the names of those who stamped themselves upon their time for good or evil, and thus the capital of the Eastern Empire owes its second birth to one whose glorious name is writ large upon the scroll of fame—to Constantine the Great. Second only to Constantine in this succession of rulers of the Eastern Empire comes Theodosius I, also called Great, and rightly so, for Constantinople owes to him a debt almost as great as to the second founder of the Imperial City. Constantine gave to this city a new lease of life, and Theodosius insured it against capture by assault for many centuries; for all those strong defences, the remains of which, some broken beyond recognition, others practically intact, extend from the Golden Gate to the Golden Horn, are a lasting monument to the Theodosian dynasty.

This Golden Gate itself is said to have been erected by Theodosius to celebrate his victory over a formidable rival; and to enter fully into sympathy with the great incidents this monument has witnessed, let us take note of the events that led Theodosius both to the Imperial Purple and the towering place he holds in the history of the world.

The final separation into East and West of Rome's

The Walls of Constantinople

Imperial power had not yet taken place, and Gratian was emperor. The latter years of his reign were hard and full of troubles. Northern Barbarians ravaged the provinces of Rome at their will, and none seemed capable of checking their savage onslaughts. The legions of the Roman army had time after time failed of their old tradition, and had so often been vanquished that they held their foes to be invincible. Fiercest of all these fierce foemen were the Goths, and it was they who caused the most distress. Valens had fallen in the battle of Hadrianople, and with him two-thirds of the Roman army; the rest had barely effected their escape under cover of night. The Roman Empire was in sore straits; the Goths were flushed with their victory, and likely to take advantage of it.

Five months after the death of Valens the Emperor Gratian did a deed perhaps unparalleled. He sent for Theodosius, presented him to the troops, who acclaimed him as Augustus, and invested him with the Imperial purple. The strangeness of this act lies in the history that precedes it. Theodosius the Elder, father of the new emperor, had but three years before been put to death unjustly and with ignominy by Gratian's orders, and his son banished. So Gratian's messengers found Theodosius managing his estates in

The Golden Gate

Spain. They gave him their message, and forthwith the emperor-elect proceeded to his new duties imposed on him by one whose keen discernment found the right man in the time of need, and whose sense of right had sought the way towards redeeming a terrible injustice.

Theodosius was thirty-three years of age when he ascended the throne of the eastern division of the Roman Empire. In grace and manly beauty, in his qualities of heart and intellect, contemporaries held him to outshine Trajan. Like other military heroes—Alexander, Hannibal and the second Africanus—he had been trained young in the profession of arms under the stern discipline of his own father. Even at this early age he had gained renown for valour in the field, where his experiences had been many and varied. He had fought against the Scots in their inclement climate, had heard the war-cry of the Saxons echoing among the primeval forests of Germany, and faced the Moors under the fierce power of southern suns.

He was now called upon to meet Rome's most dreaded foes, those mighty Goths, who, as their king said, drove the Roman legions like sheep before them. Theodosius showed no impetuous haste to gain new laurels for his own adornment. Rather, he bided his

The Walls of Constantinople

time, placed his troops cunningly, and kept himself so well informed that whenever an opportunity offered of attacking a small force of the enemy in superior numbers, or from some vantage ground, he would seize it, and always proved successful. Thus he restored the confidence of his troops, who now no longer believed the Goths to be invincible. In this manner Theodosius had already earned his title as Great as a firm and faithful servant of the Republic.

His statecraft helped him further in his plans for the welfare of the Empire, of which a considerable portion was now under his control, for Dacia and Macedonia were added to the Eastern Empire, which consisted then of Thrace, Asia and Egypt.

The death of Fritigern, who had held together the Barbarian alliance of Eastern and Western Goths, Huns and Alani, was another factor which Theodosius knew well how to take into account. Once the bonds of the alliance loosened, and the different parties to it went different ways, the jealousy of Ostrogoths and Visigoths revived, and made it possible to win the services of one or other discontented leader. The aged Athanaric collected many of Fritigern's subjects round him, and with them listened to a fair proposal of an honourable and advantageous treaty. Theodosius met him outside the city walls, invited him to enter, and here entertained him with the confidence of a friend and the magnificence of a monarch. Athanaric marvelled at all the wondrous things he saw, and, according to the chronicler Jornandes, exclaimed, "Indeed, the Emperor of the Romans is a god upon earth; and the presumptuous man who dares to lift his hand against him is guilty of his own blood."

The Gothic king did not live long to enjoy the friendship of Theodosius, though his death was probably of greater advantage to the Emperor than his alliance might have proved to be. Athanaric was buried with all proper ceremony, a monument was erected to his memory, and his whole army enlisted under the standard of the Roman Empire. In consequence of the submission of so great a body as the Visigoths, other independent chieftains followed, and four years had barely elapsed since the defeat and death of Valens when the final and complete capitulation of the Goths was an accomplished fact.

The Ostrogoths, however, went their own way. They left the banks of the Danube to visit other countries, where, having made themselves extremely unpopular, they returned after many years to their former haunts, reinforced by many of the fiercest warriors of Germany and Scythia. Theodosius, by skilful tactics, brought about their destruction. His

The Walls of Constantinople

spies had spread among the Goths a rumour that the Roman camp could, on a certain night, be easily taken by surprise. One moonless night the whole multitude of Goths hastily embarked in 3000 dug-outs, and set out to reach the southern bank of the river, certain of finding an easy landing and assailing an unguarded camp. But they found an insuperable obstacle in a triple line of vessels strongly bound one to another; and while they yet struggled to find a way out of this difficulty, a fleet of galleys bore down the stream upon them, vigorous rowing giving them irresistible impetus. The valour of the Barbarians was all in vain; Alatheus their king perished in the fray, together with the flower of his army, either by the swords of the Romans or in the waters of the Danube. Those who escaped surrendered and became Roman subjects.

The Goths soon settled in the Empire, the Visigoths in Thrace, the remnant of the Ostrogoths in Phrygia and Lydia, while many took service under the Roman eagles. They were allowed to retain their own free government, but the royal dignity was abolished, and their kings and chieftains ranked as generals, to be appointed and removed at the royal pleasure. Under the name of Fœderati 40,000 Goths were maintained for the perpetual service of the East; they were distinguished by their golden collars, liberal pay, and

The Golden Gate

licentious privileges. So here we find the walls of Constantinople guarded by its former enemies, while the population lose more and more of the military spirit of ancient Rome. No love was lost, we fancy, between the citizens of Old Byzantium and these haughty Barbarians. Indeed, one old chronicler relates how the city was deprived for half a day of the public allowance of bread, to expiate the murder of a Gothic soldier. There is no record of how many Greek citizens a Barbarian guardsman was allowed to murder if he thought fit to do so; probably statistics would be striking.

No doubt the idea was that a fine blend of races might thus be induced, an idea that has occurred to other conquerors and has not always proved successful. So in this case: the Goths, it was supposed, would acquire habits of industry and obedience, while Christianity and education smoothed over the very apparent roughness of their disposition.

Though gratitude is a virtue that is generally attributed to Barbarians and denied to highly civilized races, the Goths made no signal display of it, and from time to time deserted in large bodies to make the neighbouring provinces unhappy. Thus on one occasion, when their services were particularly required in a civil war against Maximus, the Goths considered that the time had come for a little private entertainment. They therefore retired to the morasses of Macedonia, and indulged in a course of quite unnecessary outrage. It required the presence of the Emperor himself to persuade them to return to their allegiance. Some attributed these alarums and excursions to the sudden rise of the barbaric passion, to which a strong, undisciplined race is always prone. But others maintain that there was much method in their madness, and that these outbursts were the result of deep and long-premeditated design, for it was generally believed that when the Goths had signed the treaty binding them to peace and service, they had previously sworn never to keep faith with Romans, and to neglect no opportunity favourable to revenge. The second opinion seems to have been formed on quite sufficient grounds, and one occurrence tends to prove it. Two factions there were among the Goths: the one led by Fravitta, a valiant, honourable youth, considered itself friendly to peace, to justice, and to the interests of Rome; the other and more numerous faction asserted its independence under a fierce and passionate leader—Priulf.

On one occasion, when a solemn festival had gathered all the great officers of State together, Priulf and Fravitta, having according to the custom of their race duly overheated themselves with wine, forgot the usual restraints of discretion and respect, and betrayed in the presence of Theodosius the secrets of their domestic disputes. The meeting ended in tumult. Theodosius was compelled to dismiss his guests. Fravitta, exasperated by his rival's insolence, followed him, drew his sword and slew him. Priulf's companions flew to arms, and in their superior numbers would have overcome Fravitta and his followers had not the Imperial guard stepped in to save him.

Now Author and Artist are at variance in their views of the incident just related. The Author looks upon the subject from a lofty pedestal built of historic facts, and has just given this account of an abrupt and unpleasant ending to a dinner-party in order to shake his head reprovingly over the want of self-control exhibited by the invited Gothic guests. He would also point to the degeneracy of the Roman Empire, when such scenes could be enacted in the presence of the Emperor. What was the Lord High Guest-Inviter about to ask Fravitta and Priulf to meet? He should have known that they would quarrel in their cups, and have sent out his separate invitations for two repasts, though perhaps for consecutive evenings. And the Lord High Bottle-Washer? Surely one in his exalted station should have recognized from long

The Walls of Constantinople

experience the first symptoms, and substituted something less stimulating than the blood of the grape on the third or fourth circuit of the decanter. For surely concoctions equally tasty and considerably under proof must have been known to "the Trade" in those ages of gastronomic culture. However, matters turned out as recorded, and the Artist revels in the episode. The Church's solemn feast had been duly observed that morning; no doubt the Goths had taken part in church parade, and had, as usual, failed to be sufficiently impressed with the solemnity of the occasion. Then all the great ones proceeded to the palace, and, already chafing at the length of the sermon, grew yet more impatient at the delay of dinner while waiting in some ante-room. The Emperor Theodosius Augustus enters, and a stir goes through the assembly. A kind word here and there in Latin, Greek, or some barbaric tongue as the kind-hearted Emperor recognizes a familiar face, and then into the banqueting-hall—a lofty, spacious apartment, with arched windows looking out to sea.

As to the fare—the Artist is no expert, but would suggest that the festive board groaned, like all boards do on such occasions, beneath a quite superfluous amount of all the food-stuffs then available. No doubt at first the strict decorum of a court was carefully observed, and the weather or the latest scandal discussed in a duly Christian spirit; but after a while a louder laugh would strike a stronger, healthier note in the clangour of the table-talk, till all of a sudden angry voices rose and all the courtiers stared aghast at two Barbarians gloriously drunk and quarrelling across the very presence of Augustus. The sequel, too, seems quite appropriate to the Artist, and he can silence criticism by pointing back but one short century in the life of his own beloved country. Mention was made of Maximus just now, and it was he who gave to the Porta Aurea its origin—for had he not risen as rival against the power of Rome Theodosius would not have taken the field, vanquished him and erected this triumphal arch in memory of his victory. And, indirectly again, this arch owes its origin to Britain, for there it was that the trouble first arose like a small cloud over the Western seas.

A native of Spain, a fellow-countryman of Theodosius and his rival as a soldier, Maximus won golden opinions from the garrison of Britain, the province he was called upon to govern. The legions stationed in Britain had already earned the reputation of being the most arrogant and presumptuous of all the Roman forces; the country itself, by its isolation, fostered the spirit of revolt and justified the image Bossuet, whom

The Walls of Constantinople

we imagine smarting from his latest channel crossing, gives: "Cette isle, plus orageuse que les mers qui environnent."

So Maximus rose as rival to the throne, and some say that against his better judgment he was compelled to accept the Purple. The youth of Britain crowded to his standard, and he invaded Gaul with a naval and military force that could be likened to an emigration. Gratian, in his residence at Paris, became alarmed at this hostile approach, and found himself deserted when he tried to rally his forces, for the armies of Gaul received Maximus with joyful acclamations. The Emperor of the West was forced to flee, for even those troops whose stations attached them immediately to his person deserted to the enemy. So Maximus pursued his triumphant way, leaving Britons behind him as colonists in Bretagne, where it is said that their descendants endure to this day.

A romantic legend attaches to this tale of conquest. The whole emigration from Britain consisted of 30,000 soldiers and 100,000 plebeians, who settled in Bretagne. In a spirit of rare patriotism the brides of these settlers left England under special convoy of St. Ursula, 11,000 noble and 60,000 plebeian maidens, but they mistook their way. They eventually landed at Cologne, and there were cruelly slain by Huns. A window in

The Golden Gate

Cologne Cathedral commemorates this martyrdom, so all doubts on the subject are dispelled for ever.

Theodosius was unable, for reasons of State, to avenge the murder of his benefactor Gratian, but as time went on the rivalry between him and Maximus became intolerable. One or the other had to make way, and it was Maximus who succumbed. Then it was that this triumphal arch, this Porta Aurea, came to be erected, to stand as a perpetual monument to one who ranks with Constantine the Great in the romantic history of Constantinople.

Nearly three centuries later another Emperor, Heraclius, entered in triumph through this gateway, on his return from the Persian wars. One hundred years later Constantine Copronymus followed through these golden arches, after defeating the Bulgarians. Then came Theophilus in the middle of the ninth century, to celebrate his hard-won victories over the Saracens. Basil I, the Macedonian, followed, and of his first acquaintance with the Golden Gate mention will be made hereafter. Then Basil II of that name, called Bulgaroktonos, for he wreaked savage vengeance on the Bulgarians who had dared to disturb his peace. A weird, romantic figure this of Basil, we have had a glimpse of him when telling of those dark influences

The Walls of Constantinople

that coloured his earliest days. Those days in the Palace of Justinian when Theophane, his mother, worked wickedness, can have had but the worst effect on a character like his. Learning and all the gentler arts and crafts he heartily despised, and cared for nothing but military glory. He first drew sword against two domestic enemies, Phocas and Sclerus, two veteran generals who rendered insecure his tenure of the Purple. He subdued them both. Then he turned against the Saracens, proved successful, and as has been said already, vanquished the Bulgarians. In spite of his achievements in the field Basil did not gain the affection of his people. He was one of those mournful figures that flit from time to time across the pages of history. His only virtues were courage and patience, but they were counterbalanced by a tameless ferocity. A mind like his in such an age lends a ready ear to the dreariest superstition, and after the first licence of his youth, his life in the field and in the palace was devoted to the penance of a hermit. He wore the monastic habit under his robes or armour, and imposed upon himself vows of abstinence from all the lusts of the flesh.

His martial spirit urged him to embark in person on a holy war against the Saracens of Sicily, but death prevented him. He was then in his sixty-eighth year,

The Golden Gate

and left the world blessed by the priests but cursed by his people.

Another in this glittering pageant that passes through the Golden Gate in triumph is John Zimisces the Armenian, whom our travellers first saw in that dark night under the windows of Justinian's palace. His life was spent almost entirely in the field, and he well deserved the triumph that awaited him on his return to Constantinople after defeating both the Saracens and Russians.

The last of all the Emperors to whom triumphal entry through the Golden Gate was accorded was Michael Palæologus, in August 1261. It is not easy to discover why this honour should have been shown him, for he had achieved no renown in his endeavour to regain his own. No doubt the people gladly welcomed back one of the former race of rulers, not only because like most people they wanted a change, but because that change could not possibly be for the worse, inasmuch as they had suffered grievously for more than half-a-century under the rule imposed on them by the Latins, and were willing to accept any possible alternative. Baldwin, the last of the Latin emperors, had fled, and Michael Palæologus entered Constantinople only twenty days after the expulsion of the Latins. The Golden Gate was thrown open on

The Walls of Constantinople

his approach, he dismounted, and on foot meekly followed the miraculous image of Mary the Conductress into the city as far as the Cathedral of St. Sophia.

But Michael's joy at entering the capital was marred by the sights that met his eye. Whole streets had been consumed by fire, no signs of trade or industry were to be seen, and even his palace was in a state of desolation, grimy with smoke and dirt and stripped of every ornament.

Standing inside the enclosure we look up at the Golden Gate—the stones and brick that block up the three arches fade away, and in their place stand the gleaming gates that helped to give it its name. A surging mass of people moves excitedly around us pressing forward towards the entrance. A body of troops appears: big men, of fairer skins than those who form the crowd, clear with long-handled spears a roadway, thrusting aside with undisguised contempt the over-curious spectators. Scowls and glances of resentment vanish as sounds of an approaching multitude, accompanied by martial music, are heard proceeding from the plain outside the gate. Here they come! and already in a golden haze the pageant seems to move towards us. Huns and Alani, the light cavalry trained by Theodosius, on wiry horses, shaggy, savage-looking men, they hurry on, followed by

The Golden Gate

sturdy, heavy-treading infantry, stout warriors clad in skins of animals, with here and there a touch of finer stuff, betraying them not all unused to the refinements of the Empire's capital. They surround him whom they are pleased to call master, the Roman Emperor. And then comes endless misery, unchronicled and long-forgotten—the captives taken in the wars. Red-headed Celts and fair-haired Saxons, swarthy Moors and Saracens with desperate, flashing eyes. Among the captives big-limbed Slavs, and then more troops, some in the primitive costume of their native wilds, others in armour of all periods.

Thus passes this glorious array—Emperors on horseback or in chariots, their guards and soldiery, captives and slaves both men and women, trophies and spoils of war. In these few minutes while we watch, the triumphs of seven centuries of Empire rise up before us and fade away into that general oblivion which so few men survive, and even those often, as it seems, only by some chance or trick of fortune.

Thousands and tens of thousands have passed this way in their brief hour of victory, have made the heavens ring with their deeds, that lived a day or two in memory, and then have silently moved onwards into the place of forgotten things. The vision passes

The Walls of Constantinople

and leaves us but a name or two by which we may remember what greatness and glory have swept by.

The gilded splendour of the gates is dimmed, the stones and bricks resume their place within the arches, and here before us stands that hoary ruin grey with age, lichen-covered and festooned with ivy, while rank weeds spring up round its foundation and flowering bushes form its ramparts—the Triumphal Arch of Theodosius—the Golden Gate.

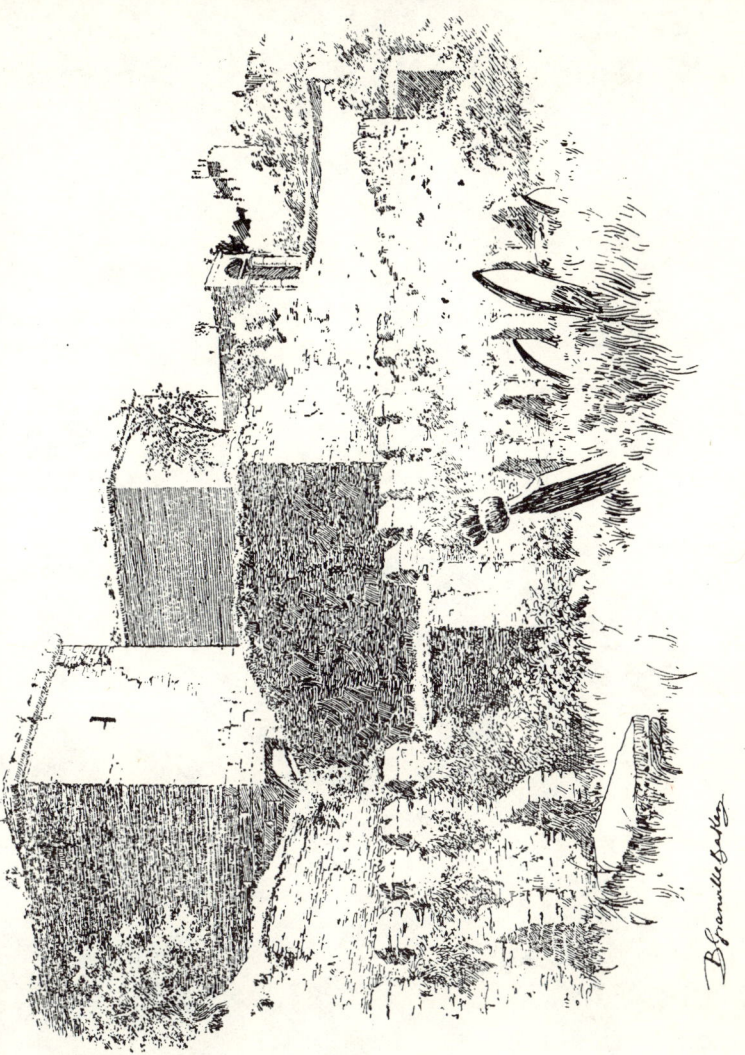

THE APPROACH TO THE GOLDEN GATE
FROM NORTH WEST.

Here before us stands that hoary ruin, grey with age, lichen-covered and festooned with ivy—the Triumphal Arch of Theodosius—the Golden Gate.

CHAPTER VII

THE GOLDEN GATE (*continued*)

The Golden Gate was from time to time thrown open for other purposes than to admit a conqueror. Persons of note who sought audience of the Emperor have passed in through it, and their mission was in the service of another victor, they came in the name of Him who overcame Death. Among these was Pope Constantine, who came to confer with that Justinian II whose acquaintance we made some chapters back. Another Emperor whose history is familiar to our travellers, Basil II, admitted the Legate of Pope Hadrian into the city underneath the same portals.

And yet another solemn procession moves in at the Gates while we watch. No blare of trumpet, no martial sound of clashing arms, no steady, resolute footsteps, scurry of horses or the grinding noise of chariot wheels marks the progress of this host of shadows. It moves slowly, to the rhythm of a solemn chant that rises into a more rapturous cadence from time to time; moves through the crowds of kneeling

The Walls of Constantinople

figures with bared heads and eyes lowered to the ground that they may not see the glory of that which is passing, for is it not the sacred Icon, the Icon of Christ brought from Edessa to find Sanctuary in the Church of St. Sophia?

Christianity owes much to the personality of the first Eastern Emperors to Constantine, the first Augustus to be baptized into that faith, and again to Theodosius I, the ardent champion of the Cross.

Until the reign of this great Emperor the ancient faith of Rome still lived on, both in that city and in the provinces. An altar to victory accompanied the Roman legions in the field, the higher officers of State in many cases laid claim to the title of pontifex and presided over the old religious rites while the majority of the Roman Senate still adhered to the polytheistic tenets of the old faith. The Emperor Gratian, fired by the zeal of Ambrose, banished once and for all the Altar of Victory from the Roman Senate. This led to a heated controversy, which was decided by Theodosius. Returning to Rome "with all his blushing honours thick upon him," the Emperor proposed at a full meeting of the Senate the momentous question: Shall the worship of Jupiter or that of Christ be the religion of the Romans?

In the Roman republic of those days it was not

The Golden Gate

expedient to gainsay a victorious Emperor, so by a majority of the Senate Jupiter was condemned and degraded. Thus when we witnessed the triumphal entry of Theodosius the Great into Constantinople by the Golden Gate, the gods of ancient Rome, unseen by us, were fastened to his chariot wheels.

Theodosius was first of all a soldier, and though born of Christian parents he did not embrace the Faith until towards the end of the first year of his reign, when a severe illness carried conviction to the Imperial heart. He received the sacrament of baptism before he again took the field against the Goths, at the hands of Acholius, the Orthodox Bishop of Thessalonica.

Once convinced of the beauty of the Faith, and sure of the unfailing aid the Church affords, Theodosius acted as a soldier and a convert usually does. No room for the doubts and fears of others, he had found the sure haven of his soul, and all his people must needs be categorically instructed in the right way. On ascending from the holy font he issued an edict which must be given word for word. "It is our pleasure that all the nations which are governed by our clemency and moderation should steadfastly adhere to the religion which was taught by St. Peter to the Romans, which faithful tradition has preserved; and which is now professed by the Pontiff Damarcus and

The Walls of Constantinople

by Peter, Bishop of Alexandria, a man of apostolic holiness. According to the discipline of the Apostles and the Doctrine of the Gospel, let us believe the sole Deity of the Father, the Son and the Holy Ghost, under an equal Majesty and a pious Trinity. We authorize the followers of this doctrine to assume the title of Catholic Christians, and as we judge that all others are extravagant madmen, we brand them with the infamous name of Heretics, and declare that their conventicles shall no longer usurp the respectable appellation of Churches. Besides the condemnation of Divine Justice, they must expect to suffer the severe penalties, which our authority, guided by heavenly wisdom, shall think proper to inflict upon them." So we find little room in Byzantium for the Nonconformist conscience, or, indeed, for any other save that of the ruler himself.

Like a soldier Theodosius adhered to his opinions, and all argument from other sides failed to impress him. Once only was he found to show the slightest inclination to listen to another version of the Christian creed. He expressed a wish to converse with the pious and learned Eunomius, who lived a retired life near Constantinople. The prayers of the Empress Flaccilla prevented this dangerous and mistaken attempt even to understand the position of others,

The Golden Gate

and further confirmation in his orthodoxy came about in a dramatic manner.

Theodosius and his son Arcadius, upon whom the title of Augustus had lately been bestowed, were seated side by side upon a stately throne to receive the homage of their subjects. Amphilochius, Bishop of Iconium, approached the throne and rendered due homage to Theodosius. He then turned and addressed Arcadius in the patronizing tones some dignitaries of the Church still use towards plebeian children. This insolent behaviour provoked the monarch, and he gave orders to eject the priest. While the guards were executing them, the Bishop turned in the doorway and exclaimed in a loud voice, " Such is the treatment, O Emperor! which the King of Heaven has prepared for those impious men who affect to worship the Father but refuse to acknowledge the equal majesty of His Divine Son." This convincing logic failed not of its effect, the orthodoxy of Theodosius was safe against all further argument, and in no other case was he tempted into the uncertain and unsettling paths of philosophical speculation.

In matters religious Constantinople may perhaps be said to lead the controversial way. It was for forty years, from 340 to 380, the centre of Arianism, and is said to have admitted all manner of strange doctrines

The Walls of Constantinople

from every province of the Empire—as was to be expected among a population more prone to disputations than to serious thought or that activity which takes religion as a staff to guide its daily task and not as a subject for polemic exercise.

Let us return to a haunt familiar to the reader—the Atrium, down by the Sea of Marmora, and listen, without venturing an opinion, to what the men of the fourth century had to say upon an all-important subject. They were, or the majority of them would probably profess to be, Arians, and for many reasons, not alone dogmatic, would have closed their ears to the echoes that came to them of a purer doctrine taught at Rome and Alexandria. Yet they must have felt some apprehensions, for among them in their own city blossomed that rarest of all fair flowers, a perfect friendship between two men of the same way of thinking. Basil and Gregory, both natives of Cappadocia, were of one heart and mind in their endeavours at reform. They had pursued their studies together at Athens, together had retired into the solitude of the desert of Pontus, and together they set out upon their mission to Constantinople. Truly a lovely sight, and altogether beautiful, this friendship of two earnest men. No doubt the heads of those that walked the Atrium of Justinian the Great wagged as they

The Golden Gate

reflected that there must be great goodness in a right so blessed.

But a cold vapour passed over this entrancing vision—Basil was exalted to the Archiepiscopal throne of Cæsarea, and by way of favour to his friend selected him as Bishop of Sasima, of all the fifty bishoprics in his extensive province, the most desolate—sans water, sans verdure, sans everything that one could wish a friend.

Some years later Gregory returned to Constantinople to try for further preferment, and in the meantime started a tabernacle of his own, and after much adversity attained his object when Theodosius entered the city at the close of a successful campaign in November 380. Gregory had gained many adherents, and was eventually elevated to the Eastern See by the Orthodox Emperor. In spite of the unyielding orthodoxy which Theodosius knew how to enforce, the Arians did not acquiesce without a protest, and Gregory confessed pathetically that on the day of his installation the capital of the East wore the appearance of a city taken by storm at the hands of a Barbarian conqueror. No doubt the polemics that raged around the question of the Trinity exasperated the soldier Theodosius, he therefore determined to have the matter settled definitely, and to that end convened a synod of one hundred and fifty

The Walls of Constantinople

bishops to complete the theological system established in the Council of Nicæa. No doubt this council arrived at some conclusion that satisfied the Emperor, so that at least one man's mind was set at rest on a vexed question. Many different Christian sects had sprung up before Theodosius began to issue edicts, and that many of them returned to obscurity is a reason for profound gratitude, for the world has on more than one occasion proved too small for rival creeds. Still it is sad to reflect that the office of Inquisitor in matters of religion was first instituted by one of the greatest of the Eastern Emperors.

No doubt Theodosius was convinced that he had said the last word on religious controversy, that being very sure himself his people would be equally so. This, however, turned out to be rather too hopeful a view of the matter, for synods, conferences and councils followed one after another, leading to endless controversy and to no more gratifying result than a more marked divergence of opinions.

Behind these walls of Constantinople the religious life of the people showed uncommon vigour, though it may be doubted whether the general effect was one of holiness. Strong men appear upon the scene and take an active part provoking strong passions much at variance with the peaceful precepts of the Christian

The Golden Gate

creed, though quite in keeping with the prophecy of Him who asserted that He came to bring "not Peace but a Sword." Out of this chaos of ideas and ideals rises one form after another, to stand out before his contemporaries in bolder outline than historical perspective warrants. Of these one may be singled out as truly great, though it is perhaps due to his personality more than to the enduring good he did that he appeals to readers of the present day. He came from Antioch with a great reputation as a preacher, so great that people called him the Golden Mouth—St. John Chrysostom. His induction to the Eastern See was carried into effect by somewhat unusual means. Eutropius, the prime minister of Arcadius the young Emperor, had heard and admired the sermons of John Chrysostom when on a journey in the East. Fearing that the faithful of Antioch might be unwilling to resign their favourite preacher, the minister sent a private order to the Governor of Syria, and the divine was transported with great speed and secrecy to Constantinople. The new archbishop did not fail to make his influence felt at once, and his sermons gave rise to factions, some in his favour, some against him, all united to make the most of an excuse for religious controversy. As has often happened since, though on a less magnificent scale, the ladies of the parish took very ardent interest in the dispute. Some there were who approved of all he said and did, others violently condemned him and all his works. These ladies were for the most part of mature age, and therefore well qualified to judge, and many of them were extremely wealthy, which of course gave weight to their opinions.

Chrysostom was of choleric temperament and unsocial habits, the first led him to express disapproval in scarcely measured terms, the second prevented him from finding out what was going forward in those places where he had been insisting on reform. So it came about that an ecclesiastical conspiracy formed against him was all unknown to him until he found that one Theophilus, Archbishop of Alexandria, had arrived by invitation of the Empress, together with a number of independent bishops, to secure a majority at the synod. Theophilus had taken the further precaution of bringing with him a strong escort of Egyptian mariners to serve as practical warriors in the Church Militant and keep the refractory populace in order. The synod brought various charges against Chrysostom, who refused to attend the meetings, so in default this august body condemned the Archbishop for contumacious disobedience and sentenced him to be deposed. Chrysostom was hurried out of the city to a place of banishment near the entrance of the Black Sea,

The Golden Gate

but before two days had passed he was recalled, his faithful flock rose with unanimous and irresistible fury, the promiscuous crowd of monks and Egyptian mariners were slaughtered without mercy in the streets of the city, the waves of sedition roared and seethed round the palace gates, and an earthquake came just in time to be interpreted as the voice of Heaven, so the Empress Eudoxia had to implore Arcadius to reinstate the favourite preacher. Chrysostom returned in triumph down the Bosphorus and into the Golden Horn, through lanes of shipping that vied with the houses ashore in the splendour of their illuminations. From the landing-stage to the Cathedral thousands of his faithful flock escorted him with frenzied exclamations. But St. John (the Golden Mouth) was no courtier, he pursued his course with increased zeal. His sermons made him yet more popular with the masses, and proved yet more distasteful to the Court, until one directed in bitterest vein against the Empress proved his temporal undoing for a second time.

Again he was banished, and this time to the distant ridges of Mount Taurus. He spent three years of great activity in this retreat, carrying on a correspondence with the most distant provinces of the Empire. His enemies, however, were not yet satisfied, and brought about his removal to the desert of Pityas,

The Walls of Constantinople

but on the way thither in his sixtieth year St. John Chrysostom died.

Thirty years after, in January 438, the remains of this zealous, high-spirited priest were transported from their obscure sepulchre to the royal city. Theodosius II advanced as far as Chalcedon to meet them, and falling prostrate on the coffin implored in the name of his guilty parents, Arcadius and Eudoxia, the forgiveness of the injured saint.

The efforts of St. John Chrysostom proved effective during his lifetime alone. After his death the religious cohesion of a large Empire, composed of so many races, each with its own peculiar temperament fell away and the divergence of opinion on matters of dogma became more and more accentuated.

A peculiar instance of this is afforded by the Armenian Church, and the Author apologizes to his fellow-travellers for having omitted to point out the unpretentious cathedral of that community when visiting the walls by the Sea of Marmora. The Armenians took up the Christian faith in a most generous spirit during the reign of Constantine. The many invasions their country suffered under, the constant disorders that occurred there, as well as the fact that their clergy were generally ignorant of the Greek tongue, all tended to separate them from their fellow-

The Golden Gate

believers in Europe. They clung to their doctrine that the manhood of Christ was created of a divine and incorruptible substance, and therefore scouted the notion that imputed to the Godhead the infirmities of the flesh. Their priests were unable to assist at the Council of Chalcedon, owing to the linguistic difficulty referred to, so in time they became schismatics, their separation from other communities dating back as far as 552. For reasons which it is not well to enter into, the Armenians have not always enjoyed the toleration shown to other creeds by the Moslem conquerors of the Eastern Empire—gruesome tales have reached the ears of Europe from time to time, and the less said on this subject the better, for the enlightened powers that now rule over the destinies of the Eastern Empire give ample assurance that those dark days of persecution are past.

Where Christianity has gained hold over the minds of men, it not only influences their thoughts and actions more than any other motive power, but it has the result, perhaps quite contrary to the intentions of its Founder, of crystallizing the national characteristics of the different races that become subject to its influence. This leads to a definite expression of national sentiments, aims and ambitions, and so it happened when Christianity was in the full vigour of youth. Those

The Walls of Constantinople

communities whose life was lived under a southern sun, in lands where tradition and history receded into the dim vistas that hide the origin of all things, lands like Syria and Egypt drifted into a spiritual nirvana of lazy and contemplative devotion. No wonder then that the fierce onrush of those who were inflamed by Mahomed's fighting creed met with no resistance, and Islam is now the faith of those lands of ruin and golden sand.

The Western nations took to the new creed without any loss of the fighting qualities of their race; and in fact the preaching of the new religion seems to have had but little effect upon their methods of expressing their convictions on any subject, and equally little power to check ambition. So the Western Church was forced to adopt the strenuous method of the people under its spiritual sway, aided therein by the strain of stronger Northern races that had revived the moribund communities in the immediate neighbourhood of Rome.

Then the direction taken by the Western Church led to absolute power over the bodies and souls of men. The superstitions grafted on the doctrines of the Church to enhance the power of its ministers proved a weapon of irresistible force in the hands of an unscrupulous and ambitious Pontiff. The warrior

The Golden Gate

kings of warlike nations quailed before the power of the Head of Western Christendom, and one of Germany's haughty Emperors crept barefooted through the snow to Canossa, there to implore the Pontiff's pardon.

This ambition has fired the Western Church through all these ages that saw the gradual development of Europe, has led to many and most bloody wars, occasioned revolting crimes, and still acts as an incentive to the "Kultur Kampf," against which even Bismarck, the Iron Chancellor, did not battle with unqualified success. As may be supposed, the ambitious strivings of the Roman See were not directed only against the Western nations whom Christendom had reached mainly through its agents. It cast longing glances at the Eastern capital. The Greeks, however, took their religion in yet another form, approached it in yet another spirit. At Constantinople the Emperor and the Patriarch lived side by side, and were busily engaged in checking each other's authority, or offering a united front against Roman interference. No attempt seems to have been made on the part of any Archbishop of the Eastern capital to arrogate to himself temporal power. It was politically impossible, so long as successors to the throne of Cæsar were to be found among victorious generals, whenever the scions

The Walls of Constantinople

of the Imperial family showed signs of weakness. Again the genius of the Greek expressed itself in a different sense

The Roman Church laid down its dogmata, and no one was found to cavil at them, or those that did, until Luther's time, met with a short shrift and a blazing pyre. The populace of the Eastern Empire, and more expressly of Constantinople, knew none of this intellectual submission to ecclesiastical authority, and exercised their keen wits in disputations, subtle or extravagant, according to individual taste. Vehement controversies raged constantly around the mysteries of the Christian Creed, and served at once to sharpen the intellect and obscure the purity of the Faith. New sects were for ever springing up, some to be suppressed by edict of an Emperor, or to prolong their precarious existence under persecution, others to die yet more surely of neglect.

High and low entered into these contests, perhaps not always urged by the purest motives—the Isaurian Emperors condemned the use of Icons, and Theodora in sanguinary devotion restored them to the Churches. Paulicians, who abhorred all images, were introduced from the banks of the Euphrates into Constantinople and Thrace by Constantine, whom the worshippers of images surnamed Copronymus, in the middle of

The Golden Gate

the eighth century. They suffered much persecution from time to time; and again were encouraged and in fact reinforced by another Emperor, John Zimisces, who transported a large colony of them to the valleys of Mount Hæmus. Under good treatment they became arrogant, and being doughty warriors resented the injuries they frequently received at the hands of the Eastern clergy. They retired to their native land, and there were subject to renewed attacks by their Christian brethren of the Eastern fold, and by any armed and adventurous nation of a different Faith who happened to pass that way.

Asia too has had experience of a religious war lasting thirty years and devastating many tracts of fair and fertile country, an example followed by Europe nearly eight centuries later.

Thus the religious life of Constantine's great city was not without intense excitement to those who lived within the walls. After the first eight centuries of the Christian era, the interest somewhat abated, the degenerate population seemed to have lost its appetite for controversy. A definite separation from Rome had not been brought about, though it may be supposed that the Roman Pontiff exercised little direct control over the religious destinies of the Eastern Empire.

The recital of religious differences, of disputes

The Walls of Constantinople

concerning the mysteries of any faith make unpleasant reading at any time. But yet such matters have to be faced if we would restore some of the testimony of these silent witnesses, the ruined walls of Constantinople. Thus if we are to read the history their stones record, we cannot overlook the darker pages, the depth of shadows that offer such contrast to the brighter passages of the chronicles of this Imperial City.

The Eastern and the Western world were never really in accord on any subject—the bonds that united them were frail and might snap at the death of one strong man or the other, who like Constantine had firm hold of the reins of government. But the Western Empire was no more, and owing to this and the disorders that ensued in consequence, the Eastern Empire gained in importance. It at least presented a united front to outward enemies, so when Charlemagne restored the western Roman Empire, a rivalry of power seemed imminent—this marked the distance East and West had travelled on diverging roads and brought about a separation of the Greek and Latin Churches. The intellectual pride of the Greeks could not submit to any dictation on the subject of the Christian doctrine from the See of Rome; Roman ambition would not allow outlying communities to

The Golden Gate

formulate new doctrines or to revise old ones. In everything the adherents of the Eastern and Western Churches found points of disagreement. It needed but a small pretext to bring about a schism, small at this period of time but great and momentous to those who struggled through the controversy. A pretext was not long wanting. About the middle of the ninth century Photius, a layman, captain of the guards, was promoted by merit and favour to the office of Patriarch of Constantinople. In ecclesiastical science and in the purity of morals he was equally well qualified for his high office. But Ignatius, his predecessor, who had abdicated, had still many obstinate supporters, and they appealed to Pope Nicholas I, one of the proudest and most ambitious of the Roman Pontiffs, who welcomed an opportunity of judging and condemning his rival of the East.

The Greek Patriarch issued triumphant with the aid of the Court, but fell with his patron, Cæsar Bardas, uncle of Michael III, whereupon Basil the Macedonian restored Ignatius to his former dignity. Photius emerged on the death of Ignatius from the monastery which had sheltered him and was again restored to the dignity of the Patriarchate, to be again and for ever deprived of office on the death of Basil I. The Roman See had interfered in favour of Ignatius, and had

The Walls of Constantinople

become unpopular with all sections of Greek Orthodoxy in consequence. Then followed the dark and hopeless days of the tenth century, without any attempt at reconciliation between the Churches. Nothing but unseemly recriminations ensued, till in 1054 the Papal legates entered Constantinople, having laid a bill of excommunication against the Patriarch upon the altar of St. Sophia, and shaking the dust from off their feet returned to Rome. Negotiations between the two Churches continued at ever-increasing intervals, and the breach widened by the actions of both sides.

When the Western nations, fired by religious enthusiasm, pressed eastward in their thousands to attempt the rescue of the Holy Land, they met with faint support, and even covert opposition from the Eastern Emperors. And when the Eastern Empire was hard pressed by the old enemy of the Cross, the Pope refused his aid until urged thereto by one of his own spiritual vassals, and that, as we have seen, in vain.

From time to time attempts were made at reconciliation, but whether they were sincere is hard to determine, and certainly does not come within the province of this book. Suffice it to say, they failed, and now under the protection of Crescent and Star the Orthodox Greek Church preserves the even tenor of her way.

The Golden Gate

Author and Artist wonder whether perchance they should apologize for talking at length on a matter of such vital interest as the religious controversies between different schools of Christian thought. They decide not to do so, for to give a fair account of all the history or of as much of it as one small volume may contain, the strong note that dominated the lives and motives of so many generations, all struggling upwards to the Light, must sound above the universal and jarring discords.

There is yet another feature of the religious life that had its day behind these sheltering walls, its monastic institutions. The Author has views on the subject of political economy which he does not intend to inflict upon his fellow-travellers. Of a truth this is neither a reasonable time nor an appropriate place for any such controversial matter. Rather the Author proposes to entrust his patient audience to the mercy of the Artist, who has a tale to tell and may be some time in telling it. Thus he leaves his collaborator to think out the next chapter, for much remains to be told.

Meanwhile the Artist takes us back to those remote, romantic ages when Christianity was young and even more capable than it is to-day of arousing fierce passions which led to what the cynics of other ages regard as mere extravagances. He tells of Anthony, an illiterate youth who lived in Thebais at the beginning of the fourth century. Of how Anthony distributed his patrimony, left his kith and kin and began his monastic penance among the tombs in a ruined tower by the banks of the Nile. How Anthony then wandered three days' journey into the desert to eastward of the Nile and fixed his last residence in a lonely spot where he had found shade and water. From Egypt, that land of mystery, this novel conception of a Christian's duty spread over all the Christian world. Anthony's fame went far afield, many disciples followed him, and ere he died at the advanced age of 105 he was surrounded by many fellow-anchorites ready to follow in his footsteps.

The people of the Eastern Empire took up the new idea with enthusiasm, and many monasteries were erected within the walls of Old Byzantium. One of them has already been mentioned, the monastery of St. George at the Mangane near Seraglio Point, where for some time the Emperor John Cantacuzene took up his abode after his abdication. Monasteries and convents were in fact almost invaluable to party politicians of the Byzantine Empire. Emperors and Empresses were conveyed to these places of retreat, with more or less of ceremony according to the judgment passed on

The Golden Gate

their misdeeds, real or supposed, by the fickle populace. Royal Princes who might be tempted to usurp the throne were banished to convenient monasteries, and sometimes deprived of eyesight that they might realize the vanity of all things. Victorious and ambitious generals found unsought rest and quietness in the cloister, even Patriarchs have been known to vanish from sight into the " dim religious light " that was the material and spiritual attribute of those secluded haunts. Those fairy islands we saw floating in the placid Sea of Marmora held many illustrious captives within the walls of its cloisters and convents. Distant Mount Athos with its thousands of anchorites would from time to time welcome back a brother who had basked for a short time in the sunlight of an Emperor's smile.

But through all those ages of monastic life, in all the stories and legends of pious hermits and anchorites, the Artist misses any one akin to his own admired friend—Friar Tuck. Greek monks took frequent part in the disturbances that party politics provoked, but none was found to expound like him, his doctrine of Christian Socialism with the aid of a stout quarterstaff.

And of the artistic side of monastic usefulness no trace remains, none of those beautifully executed illuminations that were the life-work of so many a

The Walls of Constantinople

skilful limner in the West. The storm that broke over Constantinople swept all this away, and nothing is left but a faint record of the site of some ancient hermitage.

Thus on our way to the Marble Tower and not far from where we stand stood a monastery dedicated to St. Diomed, and hereby hangs a tale full as romantic as any yet recorded.

One evening in the middle of the ninth century a youth, strong and active, but weary and travel-stained, approached the Golden Gate from over the heights beyond the walls. He entered the city, but not by the Golden Gate that we are now so well acquainted with, he went round a little to the north, where there is another opening in the walls, a sort of "tradesmen's entrance," for to none but Emperors or visitors of the highest rank was the Golden Gate thrown open. The wanderer was none of these, so by the failing light he entered what is now Yedi Koulé Kapoussi. He had neither friends nor money, so tired out lay down to sleep on the steps of the Church of St. Diomed. A kindly monk extended the hospitality of the monastery to him, and so refreshed he went his way in search of fortune. His good luck took him to a cousin, a namesake of the Emperor Theophilus, and in his patron's train he went to the Peloponnese. His personal merit brought him advancement, and fortune

YEDI KOULÉ KAPOUSSI, OR GATE OF THE SEVEN TOWERS.

One evening in the middle of the ninth century, a youth entered the city, but not by the Golden Gate, for to none but Emperors or visitors of the highest rank was the Golden Gate thrown open—he entered what is now Yedi Koulé Kapoussi.

The Golden Gate

favoured him again in making him acquainted with a wealthy widow, Danielis, who adopted him as her son. This youth was Basil I—the founder of the Macedonian Dynasty, whom we saw in that proud pageant of victorious Emperors passing under the Porta Aurea.

The monks of St. Diomed had no occasion to repent their hospitality to the stranger, for Basil found many ways of proving his gratitude towards his former hosts.

CHAPTER VIII

THE WALLS OF THEODOSIUS TO THE GATE OF ST. ROMANUS

HAVING escaped from the hands of the Artist, the travellers fall into the clutches of the Author, who insists on showing them the Golden Gate from both sides as it really is to-day. For that purpose we enter by a gateway a little to the north of the Porta Aurea. This is called Yedi Koulé Kapoussi, or the "Gate of the Seven Towers," and stands where stood formerly a Byzantine gate through which Basil entered the city. As we may infer from its name, the present gate is of Turkish origin, as are also the strong towers that rise up on our right. Bearing southwards, we come to an entrance in that section of the wall which faces east. We enter and stand, in fact, where we had stood in imagination watching the triumphant pageants of former ages defiling past us. We may enter one of the strong towers, the shape of which is familiar to all who have visited Roumeli Hissar, and thus we know it to be of Turkish construction. A winding staircase

PART OF TURKISH FORTRESS OF YEDI KOULÉ.

We may enter one of the strong towers, the shape of which is familiar to all who have visited Roumeli Hissar, and thus we know it to be of Turkish construction.

The Walls of Theodosius

leads us to the rampart; through a bend in the wall we may look down into the interior of the tower, where erstwhile spacious vaulted chambers held the garrison while captives pined in the dungeons below.

The romantic tales that cling to all dungeons are not wanting here, for beneath this spot even ambassadors are said to have languished, though probably not for any length of time, for the person of such high representatives of foreign potentates partake in some degree of their master's lustre and may not be lightly treated. Nevertheless, the Venetian ambassador was once arrested by Achmet III, when he and Charles XII, the most picturesque figure of the beginning of the eighteenth century, were allied against Russia, and Venetian possessions in Morea barred the path of further Turkish conquests.

As we walk along the top of the ramparts we see how strong these ruined walls still remain, and how much greater their strength must have been when rebuilt in 1457 A.D. by Mahomet the conqueror. And before Mahomet's day this citadel's history was a record of stout resistance to the city's enemies, for it long defied the onslaught of the Turks, who rebuilt it when the city fell into their hands. The Sultan had planted a cannon before this stronghold, and tried its strength with other engines of war, but Manuel of

The Walls of Constantinople

Liguria and his two hundred men held out until the end.

A pathetic figure appeared in 1347, John Cantacuzene, who, though a loyal guardian to his young Imperial master, was driven into civil war by court intrigues. His followers admitted him into this stronghold before he retired to monastic seclusion. He had some difficulty in persuading his partisans, the Latin garrison, to surrender to John Palæologus. This emperor then thought fit to weaken the defences of this citadel, but luckily left it strong enough to protect himself from the attacks of his rebellious son Andronicus.

Good reason for strengthening the fort occurred when Bajazet roamed at large in Europe, and John Palæologus set about doing so. The Sultan, hearing of it, sent an order that those new defences should be at once pulled down again, and that non-compliance would mean the loss of eyesight to Manuel, heir to the throne and at that time hostage in the Turkish camp.

Standing on the ramparts of this ancient stronghold it is difficult to realize the old days of stress and storm. In the clear air and sunshine life seems too serene for the fierce passions that drove a swarm of Saracens in repeated attacks against the grey walls. These fiery

The Walls of Theodosius

followers of the prophet came up from the South over that limpid sea. Yet in the seventh century, forty-six years after the flight of Mahomed from Mecca, it was alive with the lateen sails of the swarthy marauders.

Caliph Moawiyah had no sooner resumed the throne by suppressing his rivals than he decided to wipe away the bloodstains of civil strife by a holy war. A holy war, if it is to attain to the fullest perfection of sanctity, should also be profitable, and no richer prize offered than Constantinople. The Arabs, since they had issued from the desert, had found victory rapid and easy of achievement; so, having carried their triumphant ensign to the banks of the Indus and the heights of the Pyrenees, they had some reason to consider themselves invincible. Not only was the capital of the Eastern Empire the richest prize, but its conquest seemed to present no great difficulties, as an unworthy emperor loosely held the reins of government at this time. Heraclius had entered the Golden Gate in triumph after defeating the Persians. Constantine, his grandson, third of that name, was called upon to defend it against the Saracens.

These fierce warriors were allowed to pass unchallenged through the narrow channel of the Dardanelles, where they might at least have been checked, and landed near the Hebdomon. Day by day, from

The Walls of Constantinople

dawn till sunset, the sons of the desert surged round the stately defences of the city, their main attack being directed against the Golden Gate. Every attempt proved abortive, yet they held on with marvellous persistence. On the approach of winter they would retire to a base established on the isle of Cysicus, where they stored their spoils and provisions. For six successive summers they kept up the attempt upon the city walls, their hope and vigour gradually fading, until shipwreck and disease, allied with sword and fire, the newly-invented Greek fire, forced them to relinquish the fruitless enterprise. Their losses are computed at 30,000 slain, and among these they bewailed the loss of Abou Eyub or Tob. That venerable Arab was one of the last-surviving companions of Mahomed; he was numbered among the ansars or auxiliaries of Medina, who sheltered the head of the fugitive prophet. Eyub lies buried at a spot not far from the northern extremity of the land-walls on the shores of the Golden Horn, where a mosque, one of the most beautiful of all those that adorn Constantinople, now enshrines his bones. It is at this Mosque of Eyub that the Sultan, on his accession, is girded with the sacred sword of Othmar, a ceremony that compares in religious importance with the coronation of a Christian monarch.

The unsuccessful issue of the Saracen attacks upon

The Walls of Theodosius

Constantinople cast a shadow upon the lustre of their army, and revived both in the East and West the prestige of the Roman sword. A truce of thirty years was ratified at Damascus in 677, and the majesty of the Commander of the Faithful was dimmed by the necessity of paying tribute, fifty horses of a noble breed, fifty slaves and three thousand pieces of gold.

A yet more barbarous enemy appeared before this section of the city walls in Leo the Armenian's reign. Rumours of their approach had reached the city, and it was heralded by vast clouds of dust raised by the feet of innumerable flocks of sheep and goats who accompanied these adventurers wherever they went. They pitched their leathern tents on the plain and heights outside the Golden Gate, where their strange aspect startled those who held watch and ward over the city. These barbarians were clad in furs, they shaved their heads and scarified their faces, of luxury they knew nothing, and their sole industries were violence and rapine.

Finding all his efforts against the stout walls of the city unavailing, King Crum, the leader of these hordes, offered up human sacrifices under the Golden Gate. But this failed to propitiate his gods, and one day a receding cloud of dust announced the departure of these savage enemies.

The Walls of Constantinople

Another foe knocked at the portal of the Golden Gate and tried his strength against the wall in vain, though sometimes more successful in the open field. A new power had arisen on the banks of the Danube in the days of Constantine III—the Bulgarians.

Whence they came and what their origin is still a matter of conjecture best left to those whose business it is to find out. Suffice it to say that they appear from time to time and trouble the peace of the Eastern Empire, or on some rare occasions act as its allies. Their history is strangely stirring. Theodoric, in his march to Italy, had trampled on them, and for a century and a half all traces of their name and nation disappear from the historian's ken. In the ninth century we hear of them again on the southern bank of the Danube. Their return to the North from whence they came was prevented by a stronger race that followed them, whilst their progress to the West was checked by more powerful nations in that quarter. They found some vent for their military ardour in opposing the inroads of the Eastern emperors, and may lay claim to an honour till then appropriated only by the Goths—that of having slain a Roman emperor in battle.

It came about in this fashion. The Emperor Nicephorus had advanced with boldness and success into the west of Bulgaria and destroyed the royal court

The Walls of Theodosius

by fire. But while he lingered on in search of spoil, refusing all treaties, his enemies collected their forces and barred the passes of retreat. For two days the Emperor waited in despair and inactivity, on the third the Bulgarians surprised the camp and slew the Emperor and great officers of the Eastern Empire. Valens had, after the Emperor's death at the hands of the Goths, escaped from insult, but the skull of Nicephorus I, encased with gold, served as a drinking vessel.

Before the end of the same century a better understanding had been established, and the sons of Bulgarian nobles were educated in the schools and palaces of Constantinople; among them was Simeon, a youth of royal line, of whom Luitprand the historian says: "Simeon fortis bellator, Bulgariæ prœcrat; Christianus sed vicinis Græcis valde inimicus." Many Bulgarian youths are even now being educated at the Robert College.

Simeon was intended for a religious life, but he abandoned it to take up arms; he inherited the crown of Bulgaria and reigned over that country from the end of the ninth to well into the tenth century. His hostility to the Greeks found frequent expression, and he and his host appeared before the walls of Constantinople. On classic ground at Achelous, the Greeks

The Walls of Constantinople

were vanquished by the Bulgarians, thereupon Simeon hastened to besiege the Emperor in his own strong city. Simeon and the Emperor met in conference—the Bulgarians vying with the Greeks in the splendour of their display, though combined with the most jealous precautions against unpleasant surprises, and their monarch dictated the terms on which he would agree to peace. "Are you a Christian?" asked the humbled Emperor Romanus I. "It is your duty to abstain from the blood of your fellow-Christians. Has the thirst for riches seduced you from the blessings of peace? Sheath your sword, open your hand and I will give you the utmost measure of your desire."

Soon the successors of Simeon by their jealousies undermined the strength of the kingdom, and when next they went forth to meet the Greeks in battle Basil II found no great difficulty in defeating them. A terrible home-coming theirs; through snow and ice the remnant of Bulgaria's manhood struggled on in little bands of a hundred at a time, following the voice, each company, of a single leader, as they groped their way through the darkness. For they were blinded. They had escaped from the clemency of a Christian emperor, by whose orders only one man in a hundred retained the sight of one eye. The King of the Bulgarians died of grief. His people lived on, contained

The Walls of Theodosius

within the limits of a narrow province, to wait in patience for revenge. The visitor to Sofia, the new capital of a new Bulgaria, should not fail to inspect the museum, carefully and skilfully arranged by King Ferdinand. There he will find, among a host of interesting matter, pictures illustrating the history of the country. Of these works none is more strikingly pathetic than one which represents the return of those sightless Bulgarian warriors.

As after the crushing defeat inflicted on the inhabitants of Bulgaria by the Goths, the country silently and forcefully waited to regain its strength. Another century and a half elapsed after the victory of Basil Bulgaroktonos before the Bulgarians regained offensive power. During this interval they existed as a province of the dominions of Byzantium, and no attempts were made to impose Roman laws and usage upon them.

It was Isaac Angelus who lashed the Bulgarians to desperation by driving away their only means of subsistence—their flocks and herds—to contribute to the extravagant splendour that was wasted on his nuptials. Two powerful Bulgarian chiefs—Peter and Asan—rose in revolt, asserted their own rights and the national freedom, and spread the fire of rebellion from the Danube to the hills of Macedonia and Thrace.

The Walls of Constantinople

By the supineness of the Emperor these proceedings were allowed to pass unchecked, a fact which added to the contempt felt for the Greeks by their former subjects. Asan addressed his troops in these words: "In all the Greeks, the same climate and character and education will be productive of the same fruits. Behold my lance and the long streamers that float in the wind. They differ only in colour, they are formed of the same silk and fashioned by the same workman, nor has the stripe that is stained in purple any superior price or value above its fellows."

So after several faint efforts Isaac and his brother, who usurped the throne, acquiesced in the independence of the Bulgarians. John, or Joannice, ascended the throne of a second kingdom of Bulgaria, and submitted himself as a spiritual vassal to the Pope, from whom he received a licence to coin money, a royal title and a Latin archbishop. Thus the Vatican accomplished the spiritual conquest of Bulgaria, the first object of the schism between the Western and the Eastern See when, after the disorders provoked by hopeless Eastern emperors, such as Alexius IV and V, and Nicolas Canabus, the Latins gained possession of the throne of Cæsar. Calo-John, as he was called, King of Bulgaria, sent friendly greetings to Baldwin I, but these provoked an unexpected answer. The

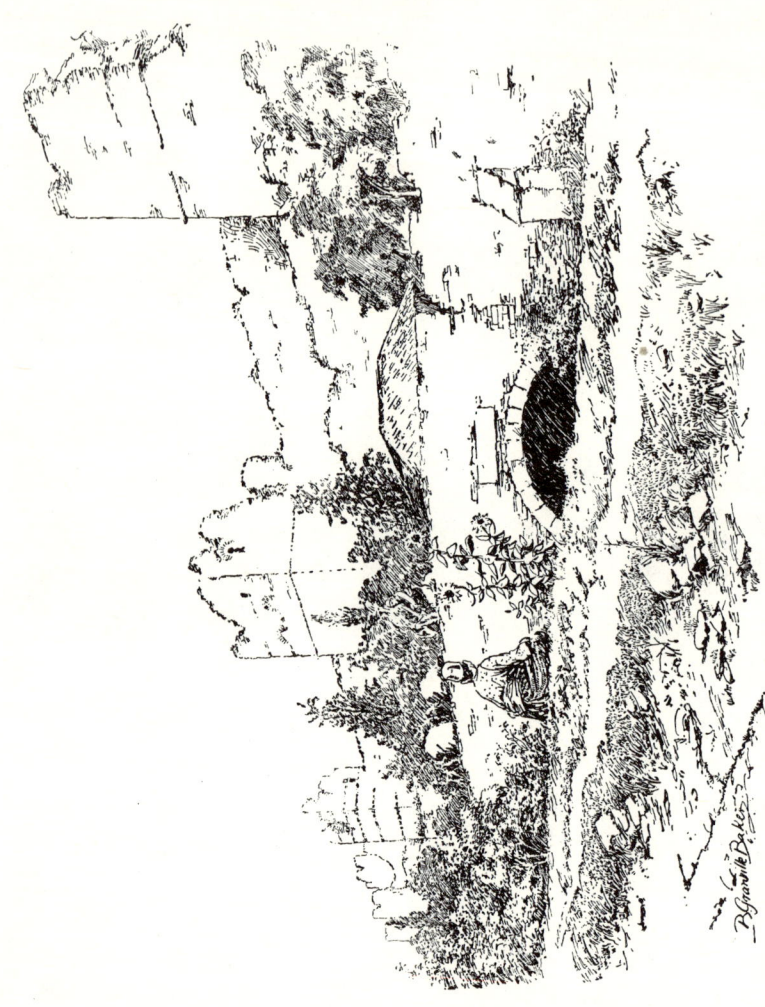

THEODOSIAN WALL AND APPROACH TO BELGRADE KAPOUSSI,
SECOND MILITARY STATE.

These are the Theodosian Walls, the proudest and most lasting monument to that dynasty which was founded when Gratian invested Theodosius with the Imperial Purple.

The Walls of Theodosius

Latin Emperor demanded that the rebel should deserve his pardon by touching with his forehead the footstool of the Imperial throne. So trouble broke out again, again war was waged with all its attendant savagery, and Calo-John reinforced his army by a body of 14,000 horsemen from the Scythian deserts. A fierce battle at Adrianople resulted in the total defeat of the Emperor, and he himself was taken prisoner. His fate was for some years uncertain, and even the demands of the Pope for the restitution of the Emperor failed to elicit any other answer from King John, save that Baldwin had died in prison. For years the conflict raged till Henry, the second of the Latin Emperors, routed the Bulgarians. Calo-John was slain in his tent by night, and the deed was piously ascribed to the lance of St. Demetrius.

We have followed the sad fate of the crusade which Pope Urban proclaimed against the Turks in a preceding chapter and seen how Amurath, surprising the Christian camp, drove his enemies before him "as flames driven before the wind, till plunging into the Maritza they perished in its waters." Sisvan the Bulgarian King obtained a peace at the price of the marriage of his daughter to Amurath in 1389, invaded the kingdom of Bulgaria, making Adrianople the base of operations; how Sisvan the

The Walls of Constantinople

king fled to Nicopolis, was there besieged by Ali and surrendered.

From that date till quite recent times Bulgaria has been incorporated in the Ottoman Empire. Now, after a lapse of over five centuries, she has again established her national identity and under an enlightened and progressive ruler gives promise of holding her own without experiencing another break in the history of the race. The Golden Gate and its romantic history has claimed a considerable portion of the travellers' and the Author's time. The Artist hopes his pencil has done sufficient justice to those glorious ruins, and for some time has turned eager eyes northward, where a line of stately towers and masses of ruined masonry offer fair prospect of enriching his store of sketches.

The road that leads us onward may perhaps pass unrecognized as such by travellers who are used to the smooth surface over which the motor races in a cloud of dust in Western countries. But let the Author assure them that this broad track, one side supplied with rough stones picturesquely dispersed, the other chiefly consisting of ruts and holes, is indeed a road, and that, too, one whereon we have to travel. Moving along we soon forget its shortcomings in the beauty of the scenery on either hand. To the left a gentle

The Walls of Theodosius

ridge, and everywhere, as far as eye can see, countless cypress-trees, some in stately groups, others in dark, jagged masses. Beneath these rest faithful sons of Islam, many of whom dashed out their souls against the walls that rise on our right hand. Tier upon tier they rise—some almost intact, others battered beyond recognition, right away from the Golden Gate to within sight of the Golden Horn. These are the Theodosian walls, the proudest and most lasting monument to that dynasty which was founded when Gratian invested Theodosius with the Imperial Purple.

We watched the enceinte of the city of Byzas grow, saw how the walls he built to landward could no longer contain the increasing population. The walls that Byzas built have vanished, and those of Constantine the Great have served their purpose, and were dismantled, so that to Theodosius II was left the task of giving to the city its widest limits. Historians of the time draw a pleasant picture of the scene when these walls were erected. The different factions all combined to help, and inscriptions, still to be seen, testify to this fact. All citizens were called upon to assist, so without waste of time these walls arose. Misfortune visited them shortly after their completion, when an earthquake overthrew a great portion of the

The Walls of Constantinople

work, including fifty-seven towers. At an inopportune moment too, for the arms of Theodosius had suffered defeat by Attila in three successive engagements, and "The Scourge of God," as he was pleased to call himself, having ravaged the provinces of Macedonia and Thrace with fire and sword, was drawing very near to Constantinople. But two determined men—Constantine, Prætorian Prefect of the East, and Marcellius Comes—called upon the patriotism of the populace, and in less than three months the damaged walls had been restored and even strengthened by their united efforts.

An imposing prospect these walls still offer even in their present state; how much more formidable must they have appeared when all one hundred and ninety-two towers stood firm and unshaken and the walls between had not been broken by an enemy's artillery or dismantled by the tooth of time! Their construction was a marvel of devotion, their plan the work of genius, for of its kind no defences better calculated to protect a city were ever devised by human ingenuity. Let us move to the very edge of the road, where there is a slightly raised and extremely irregular footpath, and take a general and comprehensive glance at the walls of Theodosius. At our feet the counterscarp which stayed the earth on the enemy's side from filling up the moat.

The Walls of Theodosius

There comes the moat over sixty feet in width. The depth when still in use is not known to us, but we know from our visit to the Golden Gate that it must have been considerable.

The wall we see on the further side of the moat, taking the enemy's point of view, is the scarp. Some of its battlements remain; they served to cover the movements of troops on the terrace between the scarp and the wall. This outer wall rises to about ten feet and tapers from a base of about six feet in thickness to two feet at the summit. From the remains of this wall we can gather that it contained a long series of vaulted chambers which offered shelter to the troops engaged in the defence, and there are loopholes facing west, through which their fire was directed. Small towers, some round, others square, about thirty-five feet high, still further strengthened the position. But the main defence lay in the inner wall, separated from the outer one by a broad terrace of some fifty feet, which served as a parade-ground for the troops that garrisoned the chambers of the outer wall, when the city was invested by an enemy. This imposing mass of fortifications stands on a higher level than the others, and here the main strength of the defence was stationed. A chain of mighty towers composed it, and they are linked together by stout walls known as

The Walls of Constantinople

curtains to the expert. These towers, most of which are square, stand about one hundred and seventy feet apart, and rose, when in their completed state, to a height of sixty feet, standing out some twenty feet from the curtain. Each tower contained, as a rule, two chambers, was built of carefully cut stone and vaulted inside with brick. Many a broken tower shows on the outside some mark or inscription dating back to the distant days of the glory of old Byzantium. On the city side of the inner wall may still be seen traces of stone steps that led up to the summit, whence other flights of steps led under cover of battlements to the roof of each tower.

For ten centuries these walls defied all onslaughts of an enemy; the battle-cry of many strange races, some whose day is done, others who stand high in the history of civilization to-day, was answered by shouts of defiance from the defenders of the city. So let us cross over the moat and look into one of those huge towers, which with their attendant curtains gave the Eastern capital its immunity from invasion for so many ages. Though appearing to form one solid mass, they are in reality built separately, so as to allow for the different rate of sinking between buildings of different weight.

We may enter one of these broken towers from the

THEODOSIAN WALL.—A BROKEN TOWER, OUTSIDE.

Many a broken tower shows on the outside some mark or inscription dating back to the distant days of the glory of old Byzantium.

The Walls of Theodosius

inner terrace, by a gap in the strong stonework, caused probably by an earthquake. This opening takes us to a place half-way between the floor and ceiling of the lower chamber. The vaulting that supported the upper floor has fallen in, but we can trace it in the brickwork that here, as elsewhere amid these walls, recall in shape and colour the remains of the defences of Imperial Rome. And yet another likeness strikes us in the courses of brick, laid at intervals in the construction of walls and towers, which served to bind the mass of masonry yet more firmly. This lower chamber, all dismantled now, and overgrown with weeds, may in times of peace have served a peaceful purpose. Access to it was from inside the walls, and the proprietor of the land on which it stood was permitted to use it for what purposes he chose. But when the fire signals that flared on the tops of convenient heights gave notice of an enemy's approach these vaults would ring with the sound of armour and the epithets wherewith soldiers of all ages are supposed to garnish their remarks.

Arms and their use, and armour to protect the warrior, knew but few changes during the centuries that these walls fulfilled their purpose. Men went to war clad in armour more or less protected according to their rank and the weight they were able to sustain.

The Walls of Constantinople

Their weapons were bow and arrow, sword, battle-axe and spear, and their tactics did not require a constant series of new regulations. Even the invention of Greek fire did not bring about a revolution in the methods of warfare, although it was used with deadly effect both in sieges and sea-fights. For many years the Greek Empire maintained the traditions of the Roman legions, but the men were not of the same stern stuff. Instead of accustoming their mercenaries to the weight of armour by constant use, they carried it after them in light chariots, until on the approach of an enemy it was resumed with haste and reluctance.

The need of reviving the martial spirit was felt by many an emperor, and edicts were issued commanding all able-bodied males up to the age of forty, to make themselves proficient in the practice of the bow. But the Greek populace resisted these commands, so when the time of trial came they were found wanting, and had to give up their possessions into the hands of a stronger, sterner race, with loftier conceptions of a citizen's duty.

With these reflections we must turn away from the vaults of the ruined tower, and leave it as a symbol of the decay that eats out the heart of all nations who forget that their country's greatness was built up only

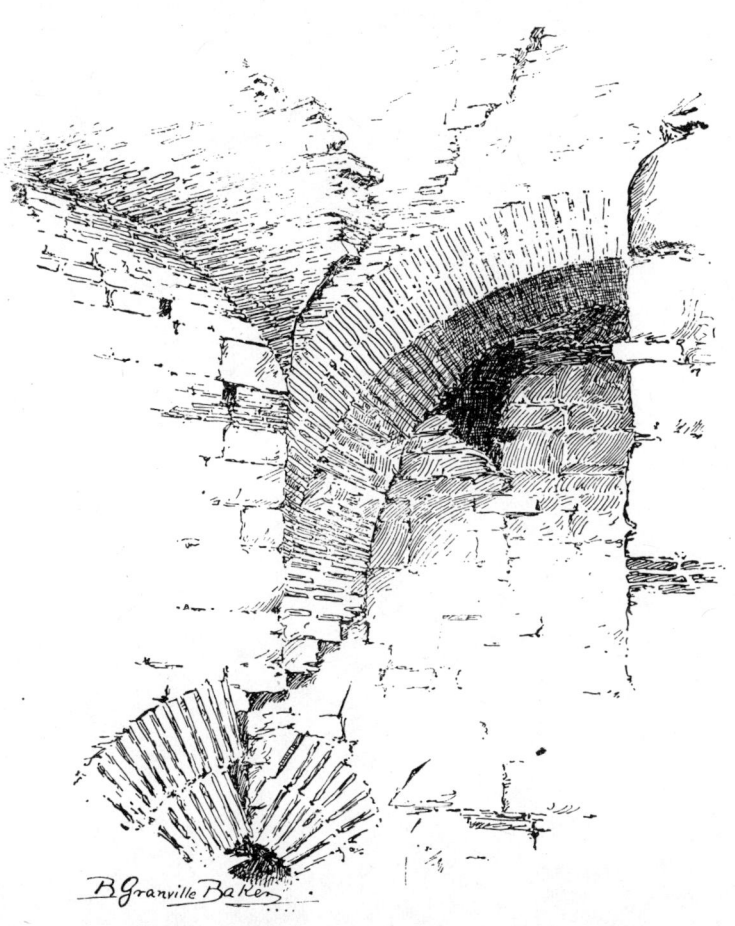

THEODOSIAN WALL—A BROKEN TOWER (INSIDE).

We must turn away from the vaults of the ruined tower, and leave it as a symbol of the decay that eats out the heart of all nations who forget that their country's greatness was built up only by the self-sacrifice of former generations.

The Walls of Theodosius

by the self-sacrifice of former generations, and that patriotism requires deeds and not mere empty words to maintain the heirlooms of the past.

There are a number of gates that pierce the Theodosian walls. With some of them we have little concern. Their purpose was to expedite the manning of the defences by former garrisons. We pass the second military gate, now known as Belgrad Kapoussi, all embowered in trees, the moat in front of it filled up to serve the peaceful purpose of a market-garden. Our way leads on along the road, which makes a curve more to northward and rises slightly.

On the higher ground groups of cypress rise in sharp outline against the sky. On our left hand is an historic spot, for here stood the Church of St. Mary of the Pegé, the Holy Spring. A road led to this sanctuary through a gate still standing, called the Gate of the Pegé, now Silivria Kapoussi. Numbers of pious pilgrims have passed this way barefooted, to test the healing qualities of the Holy Spring with the added strength of faith, and on the high festival of the Ascension the Emperor himself would visit here in solemn state.

One of these emperors, of whom we have already heard so much, was stoned by the populace on his return, and only with difficulty regained his palace by

The Walls of Constantinople

the Sea of Marmora—the Emperor Nicephorus Phocas. This gate contributed again to the history of the Byzantine Empire when Alexius Strategopoulos, general of Michael Palæologus, entered here in 1261, drove out the Latin Emperor and reinstated his Imperial master. Andronicus, that rebel, entered the city by this gate to usurp his father's throne.

Amurath II camped here, in the grounds of the Church of the Holy Spring, during the first half of the fifteenth century, and less than fifty years later, in the last scene of the Eastern Empire's romantic history, a battery of three guns attacked this point.

A few hundred yards to northward of the historic portals of Silivria is the third military gate, and at the northern tower that flanks it the inner wall recedes for a short space and then comes out again to continue in a straight line. This recess is called the Sigma, and in the quarter that lies behind this section of the wall, dramatic events in the life of Constantinople took place.

Our travellers must again return to those dim ages of turbulent history. Constantine IX had died in 1028, the last of the Macedonian dynasty founded by that Basil whom we watched as he entered by the side entrance of the Golden Gate weary and travel-stained,

GATE OF RHEGIUM, OR YEDI MEVLEVI HANEH.

The Gate of Rhegium—now known as Yedi Mevlevi Haneh, Kapoussi.

The Walls of Theodosius

but later to rise to the Imperial Purple. Of Constantine's three daughters, Eudoxia took the veil and Theodora declined to marry. There remained Zoe, who professed herself a willing sacrifice at the hymeneal altar. A bridegroom was found for her in one Romanus Orgyrus, a patrician, but he declined the honour on the sufficient ground of being already married. Romanus was informed that blindness or death were the alternatives to a royal match, and his devoted wife sacrificed her happiness to her husband's safety and greatness by retiring into a convent and thus removing the only bar to the Imperial nuptials. So Romanus reigned as third emperor of that name, though not for long, for Zoe found in her chamberlain, Michael the Paphlagonian, attractions superior to those of her lawful spouse. Romanus died suddenly and Zoe married Michael immediately, and raised him to the throne as fourth emperor of that name. But he, too, proved disappointing, so yet another Michael, a nephew, was introduced into the story by John the Eunuch, brother of the Emperor.

Michael IV died and Michael V reigned in his stead, but only for a year. His first act was to disgrace his uncle John, his second was the exile of his adopted mother, the daughter of so many emperors. This roused the populace to fury. The Emperor Michael

The Walls of Constantinople

Calaphates, as he was called after his father's trade, was dragged from the monastery of Studius, where he had taken refuge, to the statue of Theodosius III in the quarter of the Sigma. Here he and his uncle Constantine were deprived of their eyesight.

Our road leads on and, rising slightly, brings us to yet another gate, known to the chroniclers of Byzantine history as the Gate of Rhegium, a town some twelve miles distant, now called Kutchuk Tchekmejdé. This gate was erected by the Red faction, and was no doubt at one time a busy thoroughfare. Now it is know as Yedi Mevlevi, Haneh Kapoussi. It is almost deserted; two slender cypress-trees guard the entrance, through which you may see a white-turbaned hodja pass on his way towards the mosque, whose tapering minaret gleams over the broken, ivy-clad battlements.

Rising higher as we go on, we pass stately groups of cypresses on our left, and before us, where the road bends slightly to the right, a very forest of those trees guarding a Turkish cemetery where thousands of the faithful are interred. Let us step on to one of those low walls that cross the moat; their original purpose has not yet been definitely ascertained; their summit used to taper to a sharp edge, but this has worn away and we find ample standing room. Looking back the

TOP KAPOUSSI, GATE OF ST. ROMANUS.

The slight bend in the road takes us to the Gate of St. Romanus, now known as Top Kapoussi.

The Walls of Theodosius

way we came, we see a double line of walls and towers, that for so many years guarded the City of Constantine and allowed the nations of the West to evolve from chaos. The moat, once a serious obstacle to an assailant, now produces from its fertile soil the fruits of a gardener's labours. Across the road the serried ranks of cypress-trees in their impenetrable gloom, and right away, over the ruins of Yedi Koulé, the deep blue Sea of Marmora merging into the clearer azure of a southern sky.

The slight bend in the road takes us due north, though until now we have been holding a point or two to west, and across a worse pavement than before we search the Gate of St. Romanus, now known as Top Kapoussi. Beyond the road this gate is guarded by an unnumbered multitude that rest here under the forest of cypress-trees. Two roads converge upon this gate, so there is a stream of oriental life continually passing through it by day. Troops marching out to field-drill in the morning, mules and ponies entering with baskets full of country produce, and perhaps a string of camels, laden with Eastern goods, setting out for the Western provinces. And in the gateway you may see signs of commercial enterprise, small booths and stalls doing trade in a dignified and oriental way, while a cobbler sits in the sunshine mending shoes,

The Walls of Constantinople

the wearer of which waits barefooted and deep in contemplation.

From sunrise to sunset this place is full of the sounds and sights that travellers in the East are wont to enjoy, but at night it is given over to haunting memories.

Entering this gate one afternoon, the Artist had an experience which he is burning to relate. A tram-line leads from here into the heart of the city; a car was about to start and the Artist boarded it. Drawn by a horse with no ambition to break records, the journey proceeded. The other passengers were two Armenians, Army doctors, and a Turk, a young man of independent habits and picturesquely clad. All paid their fare to the conductor, a venerable Turk with a long grey beard. All but the young man—he declined emphatically. "But it is usual to pay," protested the conductor—"every one pays who travels by this tram; those effendi there have paid." No! the young man would not unbend—he still more resolutely refused. So in despair the old conductor turned to the other passengers and asked: "May this be?" "Is this the will of Allah?" The doctors shook their heads and answered nothing; the Artist, usually so well informed, held his peace, for he is no authority on the view that Allah may take of tram-fares. So the

THIRD MILITARY GATE.

In the gateway you may see signs of commercial enterprise. From sunrise to sunset this place is full of the sounds and sights that travellers in the East are wont to enjoy.

The Walls of Theodosius

journey proceeded, but not for long. The road being up, the passengers alighted, though they had paid a fare entitling them to travel to the end. This no doubt was Kismet—but it affords a striking instance of the way in which the rain of Allah falls on just and unjust without preference or distinction.

CHAPTER IX

THE VALLEY OF THE LYCUS

The sun is declining towards the west, and the tall cypresses cast lengthening shadows across our road. We may linger no longer at the Gate of St. Romanus, for we have much to see before the day draws to a close. So let us go forward along the road again. Before we leave the shade of the cypress groves the road begins to descend. Here to our left the conqueror, Sultan Mahomed, pitched his tent where he could survey the warlike operations carried on against the city in the valley below. To our right the moat deepens, and the enormous strength of the position chosen for the walls of Theodosius becomes more apparent here than anywhere. Below us lies a deep valley—the valley of the Lycus, the spot which the genius of Mahomed chose for the final assault upon the city of Constantine, and here it was that the history of the Byzantine Empire was brought to an abrupt conclusion.

By the golden light of the afternoon sun this valley

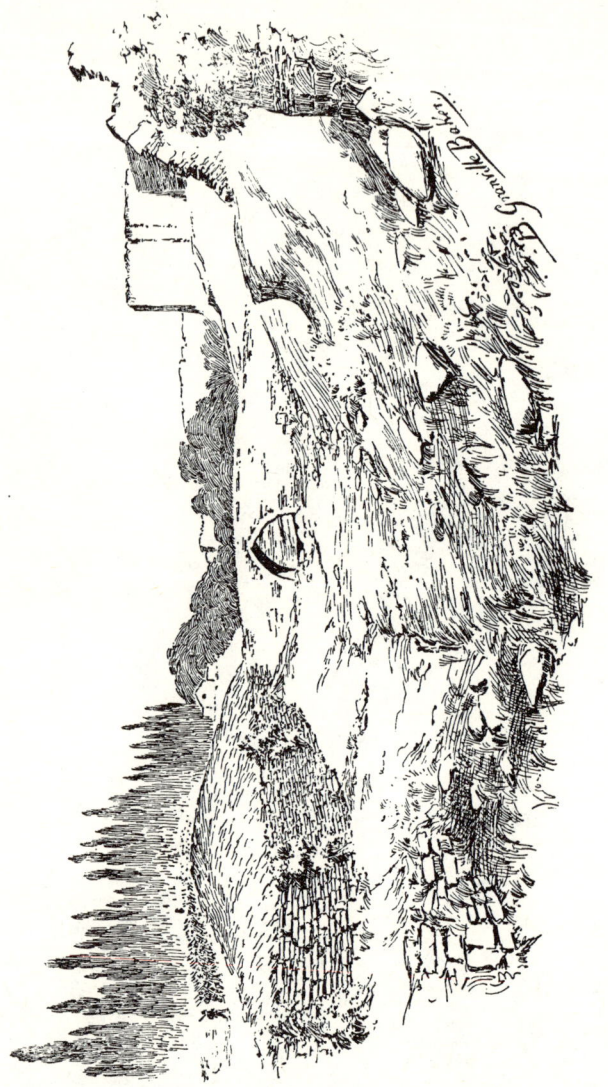

THE VALLEY OF THE LYCUS, LOOKING NORTH.

The road leads up to the ridge on the other side like a white band, strongly contrasting with the deep tone of the cypresses that crown the height.

The Valley of the Lycus

looks wonderfully peaceful. The road leads up to the ridge on the other side like a white band, strongly contrasting with the deep tone of the cypresses that crown the height. Beyond them again you see the further side of the Golden Horn, serene and beautiful, while a faint haze rising from the water speaks of industry, and shimmers in the last rays of the sun. We enter the Gate of St. Romanus for a minute and note the strength of the remaining towers of the inner hall. A few steps further, turning to the left, gives us a comprehensive view of that historic spot, the valley of the Lycus, seen from within the walls. At our feet down in the valley, clusters of little wooden houses cling to the old walls and are shaded by acacia-trees. This is a Bohemian settlement, where you may see women unveiled and dressed in tattered garments of bright colours, and little brown children wearing nothing but a coat of dust acquired in their researches on the road.

To the left the massive inner wall descends and shows a forest of cypress-trees upon the northern bank of the Lycus. The wall rises again and reaches the highest ground covered by the fortifications of Theodosius. Here stands the Mosque of Mihrimah upon the site of a church dedicated to St. George. But that chaotic mass of ruin at our feet has yet a stormy tale to tell, so we descend into the valley of the

The Walls of Constantinople

Lycus. The memories of those last years of the Byzantine Empire, of the days when the proud towers and stout walls of Theodosius tottered and fell before the black powder invented by a German monk but used by a ruthless Eastern warrior with such disastrous effect, hang so thick that former events are almost lost in obscurity.

Before the city extended as far as these walls, and ere there was occasion for them, the valley of the Lycus was a pleasant place to see. The stream had not sunk into insignificance, but still watered fair meadows. Here 3000 white-robed catechumens were assembled one Easter morn awaiting baptism at the hands of St. John Chrysostom. As we have already heard, he had just been deprived of his high office by the intrigue of the Empress Eudoxia. Yet he meant to perform the ceremony, and would have done so but for Arcadius, who happened to pass that way and ordered his guard of Goths to disperse the crowd.

Then some years later, when these proud walls were newly built, their founder, Theodosius II, rode down from the heights without the walls. He fell from his horse and died a few days later from the injury caused to his spine.

Let us now turn to the history of that race that overthrew the last remains of the Roman power. The race

THE VALLEY OF THE LYCUS, FROM INSIDE THE WALLS.

Before the city extended as far as these walls, and ere there was occasion for them, the Valley of the Lycus was a pleasant place to see.

The Valley of the Lycus

that in this valley wrested the ancient bulwark of Europe from the weak hands of the last Byzantine Emperor—the Turks. To do this we must go back into the records of the sixth century and notice the state of Asia and its relation to Europe at that time.

In the sixth century there appeared out of the East a race destined to overthrow Byzantine civilization and Persian splendour, a power destined to stretch its conquering arms from the Euphrates to the Pyrenees, and from the Red to the Black Sea. The nomad races of Arabia had never played an important part in the history of the world. They lived a patriarchal existence in their rocky fastnesses or desolate plains. Their system did not encourage national unity, concentration of strength on consolidation of resources. They had never engaged in agriculture nor practised any handicraft; their sole employments were the chase and the care of sheep and goats. It seemed that these dwellers in tents would never know anything better than the nomadic life. But a great force arose which united the groups of tribes into a nation—Mahomed the prophet—and having conquered and converted to his faith the whole Arabian peninsula, made ready with the forces under his control to spread his creed into all lands.

Mahomed's general, Khaled, called the " Sword of

The Walls of Constantinople

God," in a very short time after the prophet's death subdued the Persian army and gained its empire for his master, the Caliph Abu Bekr, Mahomed's successor as Commander of the Faithful. In the same reign Syria was conquered from Heraclius, Ecbatana and Damascus became Mahomedan towns like Mecca and Medina. Amron the general of Omar, the third Caliph, added Egypt to the new Empire, and in less than eighty years the Arabs had conquered every foe they encountered. But their power fell as quickly as it had risen. The Empire was divided into independent Caliphates, Spain, Egypt and Africa, but with the fate of these the traveller is well acquainted. Damascus became the capital of Calipha, and legend and history make much mention of the men who ruled there: Haroun-al-Rashid, the contemporary of Charlemagne, Al-Mamoon and others of his line. But the days of the Arab Empire were numbered, another race appeared in Asia Minor, coming from their hunting-grounds in Tartary—the Turks.

The origin of this newly-arrived people is obscure—they are said to claim descent from Japhet, and no doubt he will serve the purpose as well as any other of the sons of Noah. An English historian of the seventeenth century (Knolles) took sufficient interest in the Turks to write their history, and he begins with

The Valley of the Lycus

these remarks: "The glorious empire of the Turks, the present terrour of the world, hath amongst other things nothing in it more wonderful or strange than the poor beginning of itselfe, so small and obscure as that it is not well knowne unto themselves, or agreed upon even among the best writers of their histories; from whence this barbarous nation that now so triumpheth over the best part of the world, first crept out or took their beginning. Some (after the manner of most nations) derive them from the Trojans, led thereunto by the affinity of the word Turci and Teucri; supposing (but with what probability I know not) the word Turci, or Turks, to have been made of the corruption of the word Teucri, the common name of the Trojans."

The "Ten Tribes" have also been called upon to act as ancestry to the Turkish nation, but have not as yet responded to the call. It is to be presumed that the Turks are a mixed race, at least a study of the various and very different types you see leads to that conclusion. At any rate the Turks were there, there's no denying it, and made their power felt. From Tartary, where in the fifth century Bertezena established a short-lived Turkish Empire, this race spread in successive waves over the whole of Asia. One wave overran China, which remained for two hundred years

The Walls of Constantinople

under the Tartar sway. Another wave achieved the conquest of Bokhara and Samarkand, and gradually drew nearer to the western part of Asia, where they first heard of the splendours of the Empire of Constantinople. In the sixth century they sent an ambassador to Justinian, entered into alliance with him, and engaged to rout the Abari and protect the frontiers of the Empire from their inroads. They also defended it against the Persians, and defeated them on the Oxus.

By degrees they became formidable to the Eastern Empire, but their progress was checked by the Arabs, who in the eighth century overran their country and compelled them to embrace the Mahomedan faith. Soon the young race recovered its strength, and came to the assistance of the Caliph Motassem, whose nation was then on the down grade, and no longer supplied the men whose victorious arms had carried the Crescent triumphant to so many countries. Fifty thousand Turkish mercenaries were taken into the service of the Caliph, and, like the Prætorian Cohort of Rome, the Janissaries of Constantinople and the Mamelukes of Egypt, they in time assumed decisive voice in the Government.

A Turkish dynasty, that of the Samanians, ruled over most of the territories formerly possessed by the Arab Caliphs. Of this, Mahmud was the most famous;

The Valley of the Lycus

in the twelfth century he conquered Delhi, Multan and Lahore, and his victorious career was only checked by the waters of the Ganges; he was the first to bear the title of Sultan.

Another Turkish dynasty, the house of Seljuk, sprang up and dispossessed both Sultan and Caliph of the territories they had obtained. The dominions thus acquired were increased until the greater part of Asia Minor had gone to form the Turkish Empire. The city of Nice was captured to become the Turkish capital, and the Eastern Emperor Alexander Comnenus was forced to acknowledge Suleiman as master of Asia Minor.

But reverses were in store for the young Empire of the Turks; the Eastern Emperor gathered together an immense army of Macedonians, Bulgarians and Moldavians. He solicited the aid of the Crusaders, and bands of French and Norman knights, headed by Ursel Baliol, whom Gibbon calls "the kinsman," or "father of the Scottish Kings." The Turks were everywhere defeated. Nice and the western portions of Asia Minor were regained, and Iconium became the Turkish capital. Yet more trouble came to the house of Seljuk, and this time from the East, where Jenghiz Jehan with his fierce Mongols was abroad, under whose attacks the dynasty of Seljuk fell.

The Walls of Constantinople

The bearer of a romantic name, and one known to all true Moslems, now appears upon the scene. Ertoghrul, the son of Suleiman, who had been accidentally drowned in the Euphrates, was marching with a portion of his tribe, 444 horsemen, who chose him for their leader, towards Iconium, the Seljukian kingdom. He accidentally met the forces of Ala-ed-din flying before a host of Mongols. Joining forces with the Sultan he changed the fortunes of the day and routed the enemy. The grateful Sultan rewarded him with the Principality of Sultan Oeni or Sultan's Front, on the western border of the Iconian kingdom. Here Ertoghrul settled as Warden of the Marches.

In his new office Ertoghrul enhanced the reputation he had already earned as faithful vassal of the Sultan. He carried his victorious arms further afield, and at Broussa defeated the combined forces of Greeks and Mongols. The territory he had thus gained was conferred upon him, his power grew, and with it that of his race; he died in 1288, and Othman, his son, was chosen as his successor.

This, the progenitor of those who in unbroken succession have ruled over the destinies of the Turkish Empire, and whose descendant occupies the throne of the Eastern Empire to-day, was twenty-four years old when he succeeded to the government of his tribe.

The Valley of the Lycus

To great strength and beauty (he was called Kara, from the jet-black colour of his hair and beard) he added courage and energy; and, like all great conquerors, had the gift of reading the characters of men. This enabled him to make wise and fortunate selections of those whom he employed to carry out his designs.

Othman's long and prosperous reign laid the foundation of the present Turkish Empire. His campaigns were victorious, the territory of neighbouring Turkish tribes was incorporated in his dominions, and the Greek Empire was forced to contribute to the aggrandizement of his realm.

During an interval of peace, from 1291 to 1298, Othman devoted his energies to the internal government of his dominions and became famous for the toleration which he exercised towards his Christian subjects. Not till the death of Ala-ed-din, the Seljukian Sultan, did Othman declare himself independent. He did not even then assume the full title of sultan or emperor, but with his two next successors reigned only as emirs or governors.

When, after several years of peace, Othman had consolidated his resources, he went to war again, and in order to give his followers greater zest and increase their zeal, proclaimed himself the chosen defender of the Moslem faith and declared that he had a direct mission from Heaven. He thus infected them with a fanaticism to the full as fierce and effective as that which had urged Mahomed's hordes on their career of conquest. The only evil deed which may be attributed to this great ruler was committed in a fit of rage. His venerable uncle Dundar, who, seventy years before, had been one of the four hundred and forty-four horsemen who followed the banner of Ertoghrul, endeavoured to dissuade him from an attempt on the Greek fortress of Koepri Hissar. Othman, observing that some of his officers agreed with Dundar, raised his bow and shot his uncle dead. Thus the commencement of Ottoman sway was marked by the murder of an uncle, even as the foundation of Rome began with fratricide.

Koepri Hissar fell before Othman's fanatic onslaught at Houyon Hissar, where he for the first time encounted a regular Greek army in the field. Again he conquered. In the beginning of the fourteenth century Othman fought his way to the Black Sea, leaving behind him several towns unsubdued, amongst these Broussa. Othman's body was failing fast from old age, and he had to send his son Orchan against a Mongolian army, which the Greek Emperor, unable to stem the tide of Turkish conquest, had incited to attack the enemy's southern frontier. Orchan beat

The Valley of the Lycus

them, then returned to besiege Broussa, and in 1326 took it.

Othman only survived to hear the joyful news. Bestowing his blessing on his son, he said: "My son, I am dying, and I die without regret, because I leave such a good successor as thou. Be just, love goodness and show mercy. Give the same protection to all thy subjects, and extend the faith of the prophet." Orchan buried his father at Broussa, and erected a splendid mausoleum over his remains. Acting on his father's advice he made Broussa his capital, and it remained so until the fall of Constantine's city. The standard and scimitar of Othman are still preserved as objects of veneration. As we have said before, the sword of Othman is girded on each succeeding Sultan amid the prayers of his people: "May he be as good as Othman."

The romantic history of the kingdom built up by Othman was worthily continued by his sons. Orchan was proclaimed Emir and urged his brother to share the throne. But Ala-ed-din declined, asking only the revenues of a single village for his maintenance. Orchan then said, "Since, brother, you will not accept the flocks and herds I offer you, be the shepherd of my people—be my Vizier." And so this high office was instituted. Ala-ed-din devoted himself to the domestic

The Walls of Constantinople

policy of the State and undertook the first steps towards military organization. The troops that had followed Othman to victory were the same men who fed the flocks on the banks of the Euphrates and Sakaria. They formed loose squadrons of irregular cavalry, and after the war returned to their peaceful avocation and, in the main, the mass of the nation continued to be the source whence in the time of war the Ottoman troops were drawn.

But Ala-ed-din saw the need of a standing army who should make war their sole business and profession, and first raised a body of infantry called Jaza or Piade. The next corps raised were the famous Janissaries. They were entirely composed of Christian children taken in battle or in sieges and compelled to embrace the Mahomedan faith. A thousand recruits were added yearly to their numbers, and they were called Jeni Iskeri, or new troops, from which is derived the European corruption Janissaries. These Janissaries were trained to warlike exercises from their youth, and subjected to the strictest discipline They were not allowed to form any territorial connection with the land that had adopted them, their prospects of advancement depended entirely on their skill in the profession of arms, and the highest posts in that profession only were open to them. Their isolated

The Valley of the Lycus

position and the complete community of interest which united them prevented the degeneracy and enervation which so speedily settled upon every Eastern Empire when once the fire of conquest had died down.

Ala-ed-din further extended the military organization of the Othman crown, and in a manner that rendered the fighting forces readily adaptable to every exigency. A *corps-d'élite* was formed of specially chosen horsemen. These were called Spahis. Then further corps were organized, the Silihdars, or vassal cavalry; Ouloufedji, or paid horsemen; Ghoureha, or foreign horse; Azabs, or light infantry; and the Akindji, or irregular light horse. We have met these latter before, when describing battles in which Turks and Franks were opposed to each other. The Akindji gathered together in irregular hordes to accompany every military enterprise, they foraged for the regular troops and swarmed round them to cover a retreat or harass a retiring enemy, they received no pay like the Janissaries nor lands like the Piade, and were entirely dependent on plunder.

The story of a clever ruse is told of one of Orchan's campaigns against the Greeks. Othman had left Nice and Nicomedia untaken. Orchan took the latter town and invested Nice. Andronicus, the Greek Emperor, crossed the Hellespont with a hastily-raised levy to

The Walls of Constantinople

raise the siege of Nice, but Orchan met and defeated him with a portion of his army. Now the garrison of Nice had been advised of the Emperor's intention and daily expected his arrival. So Orchan disguised 800 of his followers as Greek soldiers and directed them against the fortress. These pseudo-Greeks, to give the ruse a yet greater semblance of reality, were harassed by mock encounters with Turkish regular horse. The disguised Turks appeared to have routed the enemy, and headed for the city gate. The garrison had been watching the proceedings, were thoroughly deceived and threw open the gate. An assault by the besieging army, assisted by the force that had gained ingress, brought the city into Orchan's possession.

By 1336 Orchan had included all North-Western Asia Minor in the Ottoman Empire, and the next twenty years of peace he devoted to the work of perfecting the military organization and consolidating the resources of his newly-acquired territories; in this his brother Ala-ed-din loyally supported him. Thus in the middle of the fourteenth century we find two empires face to face, separated only by the narrow channel of the Bosphorus. On the Asiatic side the Ottoman Empire, homogeneous, for all its subjects were of the same race, strong and united; on the other side the

The Valley of the Lycus

Greek Empire, distracted by constant feud and domestic disturbance.

It is not to be wondered at that under such conditions occasion should have arisen for Turkish interference in the affairs of the Eastern Empire, and a feud between the Genoese and the Venetians offered a suitable excuse.

The Genoese were in possession of Galata; their commercial rivals, the Venetians, sought them out and attacked them on the Bosphorus. Now Orchan hated the Venetians, for they had arrogantly refused to receive an ambassador whom he sent to Venice. The Venetians were the allies of the Empire, and Orchan had only a few years before married the daughter of Cantacuzene, the Greek Emperor. Desire to be avenged prompted Orchan to ally himself with the Genoese, against the Empire and the Venetians. His son Solyman crossed the Hellespont by night with a handful of faithful followers and took Koiridocastron, or "Hog's Castle." No attempt was made to regain the castle, as the Emperor was fully occupied not only with the armies of his rebel son-in-law Palæologus, but with the Genoese fleet.

The Greek Emperor found himself in sore straits and implored the aid of Orchan. This Orchan readily granted and sent ten thousand troops over to Europe.

The Walls of Constantinople

who, after beating the Slavonic army of Palæologus, did not return to Asia, but took a firm footing under Solyman, upon the European mainland. Before long the Turkish Empire had acquired a number of strong places, and it was evident that they had come to stay.

Soon after these events Solyman, when engaged in his favourite sport of falconry, was thrown from his horse and killed. He was buried on the spot at which he had led his soldiers into Europe. His father Orchan died the same year, after a reign of thirty-five years. We may date the actual foundation of Turkish greatness in Asia and its effect on the history of Europe, and more especially of Constantinople, from the reign of this able and enlightened monarch and his loyal brother Ala-ed-din. The endless possibilities contained in that strong and single-minded race of Turks were concentrated on the banks of the Bosphorus, their advanced guard had crossed into Europe and had there secured a firm foothold. The Turks were knocking at the gates of Constantinople.

Our travellers have heard already how Amurath I, the youngest son of Orchan, inherited his father's throne. We have followed Amurath's romantic career, how he restored the Empire his father left him, after subduing the Prince of Carmania, who with some other Turkish Emirs rose against the house of Othman.

The Valley of the Lycus

Amurath's rule was extended yet further in Europe at the cost of the Greek Empire, and in the middle of the fourteenth century he made Adrianople his European capital. Under Amurath the Ottomans first encountered those Slavonic races with whom they were for centuries after so frequently engaged in hostilities. Following the fortunes of Amurath, we heard the din of battle when the Western chivalry was opposed to the dashing valour of the Turk, and saw the Crescent victorious when the turmoil subsided on the banks of the Maritza. The warlike host of the Slavonic confederacy passed in pageant before us, to meet its fate at Kossova, where Amurath, the conqueror, perished in the fight.

The victorious son of Amurath, Bajazet, who first of the house of Othman assumed the title of Sultan, has been presented to our travellers. With those who took their walks on the Atrium down by the Sea of Marmora, we watched the events that marked the reign of Bajazet and felt the increasing pressure to which the failing Greek Empire was submitted. If we wish to gain some idea of the terror that was felt, let us imagine London slowly isolated by an irresistible host of the Chinese and trying hard to secure the spiritual sanction and material protection of her old enemy, the Pope of Rome. We heard the ringing

The Walls of Constantinople

blows dealt by the Turks as they hammered at the walls of Constantine's city, and breathed again when Tamerlane and his savage hordes threatened the eastern provinces of Bajazet's Asiatic Empire. When Bajazet was slain at Angora we saw how the Imperial City revived, and how hope lingered during the years that Mahomed I employed in putting his Asiatic house in order. But shortly after, yet another Amurath appeared in Europe and laid siege to Constantinople; but the time was not yet come, and he was compelled to withdraw to his Carmanian frontier. Nevertheless, the Turks were even then virtual masters of the situation; Thessalonica had fallen, sacked by Amurath II, and nothing but the Imperial City and a small tract of country round it was left to the Eastern Empire.

The travellers have witnessed the growth of the city which Byzas founded, and seen how, according to the utterance of the oracle, it prospered. They have watched the city expand under the fostering care of the earlier Emperors, and have noted how the security its walls afforded led to a mode of life which unfitted the populace for their own defence. But for the stoutness of these walls the city might have fallen long before the advent of Mahomed the Conqueror, and Europe therefore is deeply in-

The Valley of the Lycus

debted to these, the monuments of the Theodosian dynasty.

But the day was drawing near when even this massive chain of masonry should prove of no avail to check the onrush of a vigorous enemy; the encircling walls and sentinel towers had almost accomplished their task of ten centuries, and behind them a nervous, faint-hearted populace awaited the end of all things. What rumours spread throughout the city of that fiendish invention of the Latins—the black powder. Reports came in of how that foreign inventor, who had deserted to the Turks on account of ill-usage by the Greeks, had built a foundry under Mahomed's eye at Adrianople and cast a cannon of vast destructive power, a cannon with a bore of twelve palms' breadth, which could contain a charge that drove a stone ball of six hundred pounds weight a distance of a mile, to bury it in the ground to the depth of a furlong. Then frenzy seized the city, and Constantine, the last Emperor of that name, endeavoured to renew communion between the Greek Church and the See of Rome. So Cardinal Isidore of Russia entered the city as the legate of Pope Nicholas V, and with him came a retinue of priests and soldiers. The union of the Churches was solemnized at St. Sophia, and immediately gave rise to more disorder in the streets.

The Walls of Constantinople

This was the state of Constantine's Imperial City when Mahomed II encamped outside the walls and planted his victorious standard before the Gate of St. Romanus.

Though the walls of the city were stout and true, the power of the defenders was not equal to that of the hosts arrayed against them. The store of gunpowder, which by this time had found its way into use in the Greek army, was not adequate for a protracted siege, and though the Emperor Constantine comported himself as a hero should, the spirit of his people had long been divorced from military valour.

The formidable array of Mahomed's army stretched all along the land-walls, from the Sea of Marmora to the Golden Horn, and, as we have related, the upper reaches of that harbour were held by the galleys he had transported overland. In the first days of the siege the Greek garrison made frequent sorties to destroy the earthworks behind which the aggressors planned their mines, and made much progress in the art of countermining. But the serious losses such operations entailed, and the dwindling store of powder, put an end to these enterprises.

So from April till May of 1453 the siege of Constantinople continued. The Emperor and his brave ally Giustiniani, commander of a Genoese contingent, held the foe at bay, and encouraged the defenders by

The Valley of the Lycus

their example. Engines of war, ancient and modern, the newly-invented cannon, and the towers of offence well known as far back as the early wars of Rome, took their places side by side for the first and last time in the annals of military history.

Let us look down upon the valley of the Lycus, a scene of desolation to-day, and fill in the gaps that Turkish arms have made. Let us people the reconstructed bulwarks with defenders, while in the valley below and on all the ground before the walls swarm the hosts of Mahomed. Here round the Imperial standard of the Sultan are camped his best troops, those formidable Janissaries who are kept in leash until the last decisive charge. Meanwhile, the lighter irregular forces skirmish about the moat and ramparts. Down in the valley and opposite the fifth military gate the famous gun is placed—a mighty engine of war for those early days of artillery; it fired seven times a day, and for its conveyance a carriage of thirty waggons, drawn by a team of sixty oxen, was required. Other lighter artillery was placed here, all thundering at the tower that flanks the military gate to northward. Above the roar of cannon and the din of battle we may hear the sound of falling masonry, and when the smoke fades away the ruins of that tower strew the terrace. All the small towers of the outer wall and

The Walls of Constantinople

their connecting curtains have been laid low, the *débris* fills the moat, and every sign points out that the time for the final assault has arrived.

It is daybreak on May 29, 1453, and we resume our place, looking down into the valley of the Lycus. The hostile leaders had spent the preceding night each in a characteristic manner. Mohamed had assembled his chiefs and issued final orders; he dispatched crowds of dervishes to visit the tents of his troops to inflame their fanaticism and promise them great rewards— double pay, captives and spoil, gold and beauty, while to the first man who should ascend the walls the Sultan pledged the government of the fairest province of his dominions.

The Emperor Constantine likewise assembled his nobles and the bravest of his allies; he adjured them to make the most strenuous efforts in the defence, and to encourage the troops to do their utmost. He had no rewards to offer, but the example of their Prince infused the courage of despair into the leaders of his despondent troops. A pathetic scene this, as described by the historian Phranza, who assisted at it. When the Emperor had delivered his last speech he and his followers embraced and wept. Then each went his way, the leaders to hold watch at their posts, the Emperor to a solemn mass at St. Sophia, where for

The Valley of the Lycus

the last time in the history of that sacred shrine the mysteries of the Christian faith were adored by any Christian worshipper.

Constantine then returned to the palace and asked forgiveness of any of his servants whom he might have wronged. He then rode round the ramparts to inspect his troops and utter a last word of hope and encouragement.

Without the customary signal of the morning gun the assailants rose with the sun and dashed in successive waves against the walls of Theodosius. Time after time they were repulsed. The Sultan on horseback, his iron mace in his hand, watched the tide that hurled itself against the walls and towers of Constantinople, to surge back, and again to be reinforced by others who met the same fate. Around the Sultan ten thousand of his chosen troops impatiently awaited the signal for attack.

Meanwhile the courage and numbers of the defenders ebbed away. Giustiniani, wounded in the hand, withdrew, and with him the Genoese. A rumour spread that the Turks had forced an entrance at the Kerko Porta. Constantine, who, mounted on a white arab, was directing operations from the inner terrace by the fifth military gate, dashed along the rampart to help if help were needed. Indeed the Turks had

The Walls of Constantinople

gained admittance, but had again been speedily expelled. So Constantine returned the way he came, and resumed his position by a small postern-gate that gave from the inner wall on to the terrace by the fifth military gate. When he arrived there the fighting masses of the Sultan's bodyguard and Janissaries were surging over the ruins of the outer wall and over the corpses of their predecessors on to the inner wall. The fury of their onslaught beat down all resistance, and the numbers of the Christians were now but one to fifty of the Ottomans. A gigantic Janissary Hassan was first upon the walls, he and those with him were thrown back; they charged again, and fell to make way for others. In swarms they came, those fiery Janissaries, under the weight of whose tumultuous onslaught the Christian garrison was overpowered. The victorious Turks rushed in at the breaches in the wall, others had forced the gate of the Phanar on the Golden Horn, and Constantine's fair city was given over to the sword.

Thus after a siege of fifty-three days Constantinople fell before the scimitar of Othman, whose descendant reigns here to this day. And what of Constantine IX, the last, perhaps the bravest, and certainly the most unfortunate bearer of an illustrious name? He was seen at his post by the postern-gate, bearing his part

The Valley of the Lycus

as a soldier in the defence of his city. He had laid aside the Purple, and the nobles who fought around his person fell at his feet, until he too was cut down by an unknown hand, his body buried under a mountain of the slain. We may with Gibbon apply those noble lines of Dryden—

> "As to Sebastian—let them search the field;
> And where they find a mountain of the slain,
> There they will find him at his manly length,
> With his face up to Heaven, in that red monument
> Which his good sword had digged."

So, gentle travellers, ere we turn away from this historic spot, let us stand here a moment, here where the great cannon hurled missiles against the walls of Theodosius. The Lycus, now an insignificant stream, but yet so old and memorable in history, trickles away gently towards the ruined ramparts. It finds ingress under one of the ruined towers to our right. In front of us rise the remains of those walls that guarded the city through many centuries. There is the built-up entrance of what was once the fifth military gate, beside it the jagged ruins of the flanking tower, the gate of which we witnessed as the drama of the last siege was played before us. In front and all along to either hand the outer wall and moat are but a mass of ruins, and from the heights to north and south those

The Walls of Constantinople

solemn cypresses that guard the graves of the warriors who fell here, look down upon a scene of desolation. One more look upon the ruined curtain through which the built-up arch gave ingress to retreating Greeks and Ottoman assailants on that 29th of May, there in the angle caused by the wall and its southern flanking tower you may faintly see the remains of a postern-gate. There fell Constantine, the last of the Emperors of the East.

THE VALLEY OF THE LYCUS, SHOWING WHERE THE LAST EMPEROR FELL.

One more look upon the ruined curtain through which the built-up arch gave ingress to retreating Greeks and Ottoman assailants on that 29th of May, there in the angle caused by the wall and its southern flanking tower you may faintly see the remains of a postern-gate. There fell Constantine, the last of the Emperors of the East.

CHAPTER X

FROM THE GATE OF EDIRNÉ TO THE GOLDEN HORN

Our travellers are approaching their journey's end. The road leads on northward up a steeper incline than that which took us to the Gate of St. Romanus. Under the shade of cypress-trees, for here too they stand in dense and sombre gloom, we pass the Edirné Kapoussi, known before the Turkish conquest as the Gate of Charisius. Here the walls of Theodosius recede towards the city. To reach them again we enter a little wooden gate into a Greek cemetery. An attendant Greek springs up out of the long grass with a hungry leer, and though we may not understand his speech, his hand extended to us, palm upwards, makes his meaning clear. The Artist proudly points out that on all three occasions he knows of, the palm of that hand returned empty to the suppliant's trouser-pocket. A few paces due west take us again to the edge of the moat, out of the rank grass where a few goats are browsing, and from among the brambles that spring out of the crannies in the ruined scarp and

The Walls of Constantinople

counterscarp, rise sturdy fig-trees. Their grey stems, the twisted branches and deep grey foliage form a sympathetic foreground to the mass of ruins that rise beyond them, bathed in the waning light. This is the Palace of the Porphyrogenitus, of him born in the Purple.

A flanking tower almost hides the west front of the palace from our view, the curtain that connects this tower with the next one to the south-west has a romantic history. The wall was formerly much higher, and was pierced by a small gate, known as the Kerko Porta, or Circus Gate. We well remember the name of this gate as it played its part on that dread day when the glory of the Eastern Empire subsided into a heap of smouldering ruins. A rumour arose during the last day of the siege, and ran like a heath-fire along the lines to the defence, that the Turks had gained admission to the city by this gate. They did, but whether by treachery or their own valour no one knows. They were driven out again, and for a short time longer the Emperor's heroism delayed the inevitable.

In time a remarkable tradition attached itself to this small gate. The Greeks believed that when the city should again be captured, it would be by Christians, the first of whom would enter by this postern. The Turks, of course, had heard of this tradition, so when

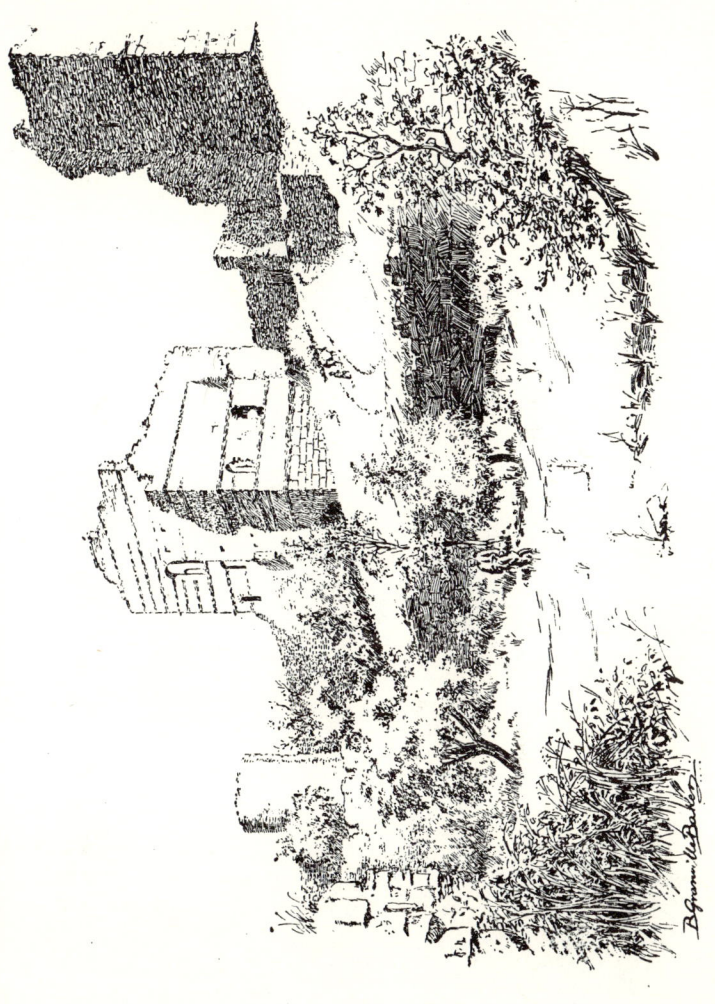

THE PALACE OF THE PORPHYROGENITUS, FROM THE FOSSE.

This is the Palace of the Porphyrogenitus, of him born in the Purple.

From Gate of Edirné to Golden Horn

a northern enemy came down upon them, when the Slavs rose in their strength and forced the passes of the Balkans, they took such precautions as their ardent faith in such superstitions suggested. They pulled down the curtain so that the Russians might not enter through the Kerko Porta, and replaced it by a smaller wall.

Before we enter by a little doorway through the Turkish wall, we will walk along what was once the terrace, and look up at the ruins of this historic palace. There are traces of an archway that seem to have connected the palace with its western flanking tower. It is said that on this archway a balcony rested. Possibly a doorway led from the purple chamber on to this balcony, for here the infant prince for whose birth arrangements had been made in that chamber, was held up to overlook the country stretching away into the western provinces, and solemnly proclaimed "Cæsar Orbi."

Entering by the doorway in the Turkish wall we get a view of this imposing ruin from the foot of a stout tower, the last of that chain of defences built in the Theodosian era. The majestic proportions of this building, despite the irregularity of the window openings, are best seen from here; and here again we may notice the remains of yet another balcony and in continuation of the legend, gather that the infant prince took his first view of the city from here, and on this spot was proclaimed "Cæsar Urbis."

To enter the Palace of the Porphyrogenitus we must walk along a narrow street with the usual little wooden houses on either side. Through a narrow entrance and across a yard, which is by some described as a glass factory, because attempts are made here to manufacture bottles out of broken window-panes, a footpath through rank growth leads to our goal. Where we are passing was a courtyard which never echoed to the ring of an armed heel, for it was forbidden to awake the Daughter of the Arch, as Echo was picturesquely called by Eastern courtiers.

Historians do not say for certain who it was that built this palace. Most of them inclined to the belief that it derived its name and origin from Constantine Porphyrogenitus, a builder of many castles, and thus would put its date in the tenth century.

We would like to reconstruct this oblong building, to rebuild the arches that supported its three storeys, and fill up the gaps that time and impious hands had torn in the mosaic patterns of brick and stone that decorated the exterior. By the aid of imagination we may succeed in this, but not in giving to the interior its former splendour. All we may safely do is to go back

The Palace of the Porphyrogenitus, from within the Walls.

The majestic proportions of this building are best seen from here; and here again we may notice the remains of yet another balcony and, in continuation of the legend, gather that the infant prince took his first view of the city from here, and on this spot was proclaimed "Cæsar Urbis."

From Gate of Edirné to Golden Horn

to those days when history was made here, take up a strand or two of the City's and the Empire's skein of destiny.

Near here and separated from this palace only by a courtyard stood yet another, a lordlier one, that of Blachernæ. This was the usual residence of the Imperial family in the fourteenth century, so Andronicus III found the Palace of the Porphyrogenitus convenient quarters when he came to wrest the sceptre from his grandfather, Andronicus II.

The history of this revolt gives some insight into the state of affairs that reigned in the Imperial City. Andronicus the Elder had devoted the best part of his reign to an absorbing interest in the disputes of the Greek Church. On this account, perhaps, he had failed to appreciate the rising power of the Ottoman Empire. According to the custom of the Palæologi, Andronicus associated his son Michael with the honours of the Purple. Michael proved an exemplary Cæsar in every respect, and his son, also Andronicus, was in time admitted to the dignity of Augustus. So there was a triumvirate of Cæsars in the Imperial Purple. But Andronicus the Younger turned out a spendthrift and a profligate, and matters came to a head when one night he shot his brother Manuel in the street. The details of this unsavoury adventure are of no moment,

The Walls of Constantinople

suffice it to relate that the shock of his son's iniquity brought about the death of Michael, already ailing, within eight days of the unhappy occurrence.

Andronicus the Elder dispossessed his unruly grandson, who, however, escaped from confinement under pretext of hunting, and raised the standard of revolt in the provinces. During a ruinous period of seven years the quarrel between grandfather and grandson was protracted, till in 1328 Andronicus the Younger effected his entry into the city by surprise, forced his aged grandfather to retire, and as third monarch of that name usurped the throne. Four years after his abdication Andronicus the Elder died, known to his monastery as Monk Authoy.

Another figure played a prominent part within these roofless halls. We have met him before, John Cantacuzene, of whom his enemies confessed that of all the public robbers he alone was moderate and abstemious. He resisted all the attempts of Andronicus III to raise him to a seat beside him on the throne, and at that Emperor's death became guardian of his infant son, John Palæologus.

In those days internal peace was not the Empire's lot for long, and soon a conspiracy was formed against Cantacuzene. Anne of Savoy, the Dowager Empress, was persuaded to assert the tutelage of her son, and

From Gate of Edirné to Golden Horn

her female court was bribed to support this claim by the Admiral Apocaucus. The Patriarch, John of Apri, a proud and weak old man, joined the conspiracy, and even assumed the claims to temporal power of a Roman Pontiff; he invaded the royal privilege of red shoes or buskins, placed on his head a mitre of silk or gold, and signed his epistles with hyacinth or green ink.

While John Cantacuzene was abroad on public service, the conspirators convicted him of treason, proscribed him as an enemy of the Church, deprived him of all his fortune, and even cast his aged mother into prison. He was forced to assume the Purple, and as rebel Emperor endeavoured to resume the charge entrusted to him, the guardianship of John Palæologus. But civil war devastated the provinces that yet remained to the Empire, and not till Apocaucus was murdered by some nobles whom he had imprisoned was peace restored. The negotiations to this end were carried on between the Palace of the Porphyrogenitus, where Cantacuzene had taken up his abode, and the neighbouring residence of Empress Anne, the Palace of Blachernæ. The proceedings ended in peace, and the marriage of Cantacuzene's daughter to John Palæologus. But the sword did not long rust in its sheath. Civil war broke out again, and finally

The Walls of Constantinople

John Cantacuzene sought refuge in a monastery, where he spent his declining years in a lengthy, if somewhat unprofitable, treatise on the divine light of Mount Tabor.

We must retrace our steps, and, leaving by the doorway we entered, let us cast a glance to northward. The moat ends abruptly, and a curtain projects towards the north-west flanked by towers. This is the wall of Manuel Comnenus, and so dates from the middle of the twelfth century. Other fortifications must have stood here before that time to guard the Palace of Blachernæ, but little trace remains either of these or of the palace itself. Yet here behind these walls, or those that they replaced, the dynasty of the Comnenians lived out their day, and they deserve a word or two of recognition if only on account of Anne, the daughter of the first Alexius, and Manuel the builder of this wall. Of these, the former aspired to fame as historian of her father's reign, but the modicum of truth which is contained in the voluminous records she compiled is much obscured by elaborate affectations of windy rhetoric. No doubt the description of her father's character was dictated by filial piety—it stands in sharp contrast to the last words that that Emperor heard from his wife Irene: "You die as you have lived—a hypocrite!"

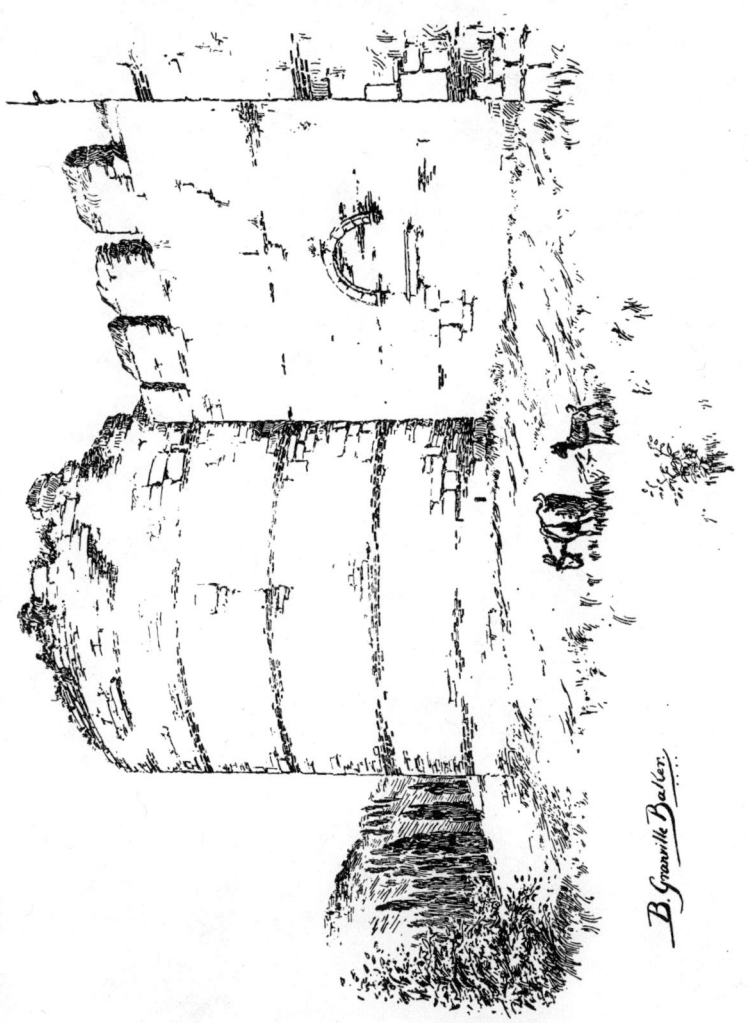

TOWER OF MANUEL COMNENUS.

This is the wall of Manuel Comnenus, and so dates from the middle of the twelfth century.

From Gate of Edirné to Golden Horn

The Empress Irene tried to exclude her surviving sons, and to place the power of government in the fair hands of Anne, but the order of male succession was asserted by those able to enforce it. The fair historian, Anne Comnena, no doubt in order to add one more elaborate chapter to the high-sounding verbiage with which she had clothed the history of her time, conspired to poison her brother John; her husband, Bryennius, prevented the design and John Comnenus reigned in his father's stead. He generously forgave his sister, and no doubt much to the edification of future generations her momentous work continued. In all the history that is recorded by the grim walls that sheltered the city of Constantine, there are but few events that leave a pleasant memory, few rays of gladdening light that pierce the turmoil of angry passions, the darkness of sordid details, the strife and anguish that largely composed the life of the city Byzas founded. And, alas! these rare events serve but to make the contrast stronger and to intensify the shadows that hang about these ruined palaces and ramparts.

We have traced the history of Constantinople through its walls up to the time when they could no longer hold out against the assaults of those who now carry on the Imperial traditions. But there are yet places left for us to visit—they have their tales to tell,

The Walls of Constantinople

and of all that remains to-day, the story of the reign of John Comnenus is the pleasantest. In him the Empire found a ruler whose days were never darkened by conspiracy or rebellion, save for that one instance already mentioned. His nobles feared him, his people loved him, and he had no need to punish or forgive any personal enemy. In his private life he emulated Marcus Aurelius : he was frugal and abstemious, severe with himself and indulgent to others. He proved successful in his warlike measures against the Turks, and astonished his Latin allies by the skill and prowess of the Greeks when engaged in a holy war. He led his troops from Constantinople to Antioch and Aleppo, there a slight wound in his hand, received when hunting, proved fatal, and cut short his prosperous reign.

The imposing towers before us stand in their great strength as a monument to one of whose bodily strength romantic tales are told. Manuel, the youngest son, succeeded his father, John Comnenus, and was acclaimed victorious by the veteran troops that followed him from the Turkish wars back to Constantinople. His reign of thirty-seven years is a record of warfare in many distant lands. By land and sea, against the Turks on the plains of Hungary and along the coasts of Italy and Egypt, this Emperor led his troops to victory.

From Gate of Edirné to Golden Horn

On one occasion when marching against the Turks, he posted an ambuscade in a wood, and then rode boldly forward in search of perilous adventure, accompanied only by his brother Isaac and the faithful Axuch. He routed eighteen horsemen, but the numbers of the enemy increased, and Manuel to rejoin his army had to cut his way through 500 Turkish horsemen. Of his exploits at sea mention may be made of an incident in the siege of Corfu. Manuel's ship towing a captured galley passed through the enemy's fleet. The Emperor stood on the high poop, opposing a large buckler to the volley of darts and stones, and could not have escaped death had not the Sicilian admiral enjoined his men to respect the person of a hero. Many and remarkable are the stories of the Emperor Manuel's exploits, but the end of his career saw his fortunes wane, his last campaign against the Turks ended in disaster, he lost his army in the mountains of Pisidia, and owed his own safety only to the generosity of the Sultan.

The wall that Manuel Comnenus built stands high, and from its lofty battlements the sentries who held their watch here must have seen many strange and stirring sights. One day in the year 1203, when Alexius III Angelus was Emperor, the watchers on the tower looked down upon a host of glittering lances

The Walls of Constantinople

and waving pennants, on white tents and the pavilions of haughty nobles, for the chivalry of the West was encamped before the city walls, and these were the hosts of the fourth crusade.

The re-conquest of Jerusalem and the safety of the holy places were the motives that impelled this army towards the East, and no doubt many of them were as sincere in their desire to attain beatitude in this manner as their precursors on similar expeditions had been. An illiterate priest, Fulk de Neuilly, followed in the footsteps of Peter the Hermit, and roamed over Europe inciting kings, princes and knights to arm for a Holy War and march in their strength to redeem the sacred places of their creed. His success was nearly as great as that of the first missioner to the Crusades, and Innocent III as soon as he ascended to the chair of St. Peter, supported Fulk de Neuilly, and proclaimed the obligation of a new crusade in Italy, France and Germany. Fulk paid a visit to Richard of England to induce him to join in the adventure. That gallant monarch declined, no doubt quite satisfied with the glory gained in his first crusade, and possibly still reminiscent of its many misfortunes; in fact, the meeting seems to have ended in an unseemly wrangle. At any rate Richard of England was not to be moved, and in the light

From Gate of Edirné to Golden Horn

of his former experiences we cannot altogether blame him.

The propaganda met with considerable success elsewhere in Europe, princes and knights flocked to the standard of the Cross on its eastward march. A valiant noble, Jeffrey of Villehardouin, Marshal of Champagne, who wielded the pen as well as the sword, has left on record the names of those that followed this adventure; there was Thibaut, Count of Champagne, with his hardy bands of Saracens from Navarre; Louis, Count of Blois and Chartres, like Thibaut, a nephew of the Kings of England and of France. Simon de Montfort, who had already expressed his devotion to the Roman Church by cruelly persecuting the Albigenses, also joined the host, and a brother-in-law of Thibaut, Baldwin, Count of Flanders, with his brother Henry and many knights assumed the cross at Bruges. The leaders of this fourth crusade, unlike their predecessors, gave evidence of some consideration for the minor details of a campaign. Instead of rolling like a vast stream across Europe, helping themselves to what they wanted in the name of the Cross, gathering strength in numbers and losing it in cohesion, these new crusaders held a counsel.

Between the solemn ratification of vows offered

The Walls of Constantinople

by these pious warrior pilgrims before the altar and the jousts and tournaments which were never wanting when two or three knights were gathered together, time was actually found to consider ways and means and debate on the many details that the planning of a big campaign entails. As a result of these deliberations, six deputies, the historian Villehardouin among them, proceeded to Venice, then the strongest maritime power in the Mediterranean Sea, to solicit her assistance in providing sea transport.

The six ambassadors were hospitably received by Dandolo, the aged Doge whom we have seen before, standing in full armour on the high poop of his galley in the Sea of Marmora. Negotiations proceeded with all the gravity warranted by the occasion, and before long the Doge was entitled by the representatives of the Republic to make known the terms under which Venetian aid could be secured. The Crusaders should assemble at Venice on the feast of St. John in the following year. Preparations could by then have been made for the conveyance of 4,500 knights and their squires and horses along with 20,000 infantry, and during a term of nine months they should be supplied with provisions, and transported to whatsoever coast "the service of God and Christendom" should require. The pilgrims should pay a sum of 85,000 marks of silver before their departure, and all conquests by sea and land were to be equally divided between the confederates. The republic agreed to join the armament with a squadron of fifty galleys, and how valiantly they bore themselves was revealed to us when we watched the naval pageant from the Asiatic coast of the Sea of Marmora.

Notwithstanding the liberality displayed by the leaders of the Crusade, the full amount due by agreement to the Venetians could not be raised, so that astute Republic requisitioned the services of the Crusaders in their own interests to reduce some revolted cities in Dalmatia. The Crusaders sailed for Zara and regained that city for the Venetian Republic. This led to some serious disagreement between the Venetians and their pilgrim allies, and the Pope even went to the length of excommunicating the victors of Zara. Pope Innocent had designs of his own, only remotely connected with the object of the Crusade, and this movement gave him a welcome opportunity of furthering his plans. He intended to re-establish the power of the Vatican at Constantinople, and fortune had placed a useful instrument in his power. In the camp of the Crusaders was young Alexius, son of Isaac Angelus. Alexius III, when he had deposed his brother Isaac, and deprived him

The Walls of Constantinople

of his eyesight, allowed young Alexius to escape unharmed. The Catholic Princes, the leaders of the Crusade, espoused the cause of the lawful heir to the Eastern Empire, and as a reward for their services Alexius had promised that he and his father would restore the supremacy of Rome over the Eastern Church.

The Crusaders landed at Chalcedon, and from Scutari sailed into the Golden Horn. The sentries on the wall saw these steel-clad warriors land their gaily-caparisoned steeds from the flat-bottomed boats in which they had crossed. What were their feelings when they saw 70,000 of their own troops turn and flee, led by their Emperor, before the invaders had found time to mount or couch their lances?

Then followed lengthy negotiations between the Latin camp and the Palace of Blachernæ, then a siege, and swarms of Franks scaling the walls that Manuel Comnenus built—and in the silence of the night that followed, when the assailants had been beaten back, a whispered rumour ran along the ramparts and grew into a sullen roar—the Emperor Alexius had fled.

The distance of time dims the awful realities that shook the foundations of the Imperial City during the few centuries that passed before the Turks made their

GATE OF THE BOOTMAKERS, OR THE CROOKED GATE.

Egri Kapoussi, formerly the Gate of Kaligaria—the bootmakers' quarter.

To-day this quaint old gateway is seldom used, the industry that gave it a name is dead; dead warriors rest under the cypress-trees that throw their slender shadows over the tortuous uneven path.

From Gate of Edirné to Golden Horn

victorious entry. As in a glass darkly we see the blind and aged Emperor Isaac taken from his prison to occupy the throne for a short space, the pathetic figure of his son Alexius, fourth of that name, who reigned not a year, to die by the hand of an assassin. A shorter reign followed, that of another Alexius, called Ducas, who in his turn made way for the Crusaders, and a Latin dynasty ruled over the destinies of Constantinople. Six Latin and four Nicæan emperors occupied the throne of Cæsar for the brief period of sixty years, until in 1260 Michael Palæologus restored the Empire of the Greeks.

Two gates pierce these walls, Egri Kapoussi, formerly the Gate of Kaligaria—the bootmakers' quarter. No doubt in former days this gate, so near the palace walls of Blachernæ, was much frequented. The walls here were submitted to a determined attack during the last siege, but the ordnance of that day was not able to effect a breach, and the guns were removed to batter against the Gate of St. Romanus. To-day this quaint old gateway is seldom used, the industry that gave it a name is dead; dead warriors rest under the cypress-trees that throw their slender shadows over the tortuous, uneven path that leads to this once populous quarter.

The high walls and towers that guarded this place

The Walls of Constantinople

have seen other watchers, who, with heavy hearts and weary, straining eyes, gazed out into the darkness. For here Constantine IX and Phrantzes the historian, his friend, saw the dawn creep up out of the East, lighting up the Turkish camps and revealing the reason of those ominous sounds that had disturbed the stillness of the night. One of those watchers never lived to see another sunrise.

Passing fair is the view from this point. From immediately before the walls the country fades away into the west in easy undulations, the gentle curves of a distant ridge broken here and there by a cypress taller than his upstanding fellows. Away where the Golden Horn, now gleaming silver in the fading light, turns to northward to merge into the sweet waters of Europe, the banks are dedicated to the dead, and here again the sombre cypress keeps his watch. At the foot of the hill, only its tapering minarets showing above the dense mass of foliage, is a holy place of Islam, the Mosque and Sanctuary of Eyub occupying the site of a church and monastery dedicated to SS. Cosmos and Damianus. Bohemund, the Italo-Norman Count of Tarentum, lodged here while the Crusaders negotiated with Alexius I. A gate led to this sanctuary and it was named after a sheet of water by the Golden Horn, called the Silver Lake.

From Gate of Edirné to Golden Horn

The watchers on the tower above saw young Andronicus go forth with hounds and falcons, to return with a rebel army behind him, and to fill up that dark page of history we have already quoted. From here, again, the sentinel would have reported the advent of John Cantacuzene with an army, to reason sternly with the Empress Anna and the Admiral Apocaucus.

A plain, now overbuilt, stretched from the foot of these walls along the Golden Horn. Here Crum, the Bulgarian king, whose barbaric rites we witnessed at the Golden Gate, was asked to confer with the Emperor Leo, the Armenian. The monarchs agreed to meet unarmed, but Leo intended treachery, which Crum suspected, and he hastily withdrew; and though pursued by the arrows of the ambushed archers, he escaped, wounded in several places.

Another Bulgarian king, of whom mention has been made, met the Eastern Emperor on this plain when Simeon and Romanus Lecapenus concluded peace.

Now let us proceed on the last stage of our journey down by these walls of Manuel Comnenus into the plain. High and of enormous strength they are still, for they form here the single line of defence; the ground offered too many obstacles for the erection of an outer rampart, and the highest point of which we

The Walls of Constantinople

are leaving behind us not even a moat was possible. Some doubt exists as to whether the wall that leads down towards the Golden Horn is of a piece with that of Manuel Comnenus. It differs in construction, and bears many inscriptions relating to the repairs which it needed. Thus the money which Irene, wife of Andronicus II, left at her death, was devoted to these walls by the Emperor. John VII Palæologus is responsible for other repairs, according to an inscription, which reads as follows (being interpreted)—

> JOHN PALÆOLOGUS
> FAITHFUL KING
> AND EMPEROR OF THE ROMANS
> IN CHRIST, GOD,
> ON THE SECOND OF THE MONTH OF AUGUST
> OF THE YEAR 6949 (1441)

Perchance this was the last occasion on which the walls of Constantinople were repaired, until the final siege of the city, when Johannes Grant, a German engineer in the service of the Greeks, under cover of darkness directed his workers to secure the portions of the wall that had suffered most heavily under the fire of Turkish ordnance, by such devices as were known in his day, and by the best of all defensive methods, counter attack.

We reach the plain below, and find our attention

WALL OF PALÆOLOGIAN REPAIR.

Let us proceed—down by these walls. High and of enormous strength they are still, for they form here the single line of defence; the ground offered too many obstacles for the erection of an outer rampart, and at the highest point which we are leaving behind us, not even a moat was possible.

From Gate of Edirné to Golden Horn

drawn to yet another sombre mass of masonry, peculiar in design, for it has the appearance of two towers joined together. They differ in structure, for whereas one is built of carefully cut stones, and shows courses of brickwork, the other is less regular, and from it here and there marble pillars project like cannon. These are the towers of Anemas and Isaac Angelus, and a counterfort, corresponding in structure to that of the twin towers, juts out in front of them amid the long grass and tangled undergrowth.

Isaac Angelus and his pathetic history are already known to us. Anemas gave his name to the second tower because he is said to have been the first prisoner confined within these gloomy walls. He was the descendant of a Saracen Emir, who defended Crete against Nicephorus Phocas, and was taken prisoner. Treated with unusual leniency for those times, he was granted large estates in the neighbourhood of the capital. His son, Anemas, was converted to Christianity, and distinguished himself in the campaign of John Zimisces against the Russians, to fall in a personal encounter with Swiatoslav, the Russian king.

But Michael Anemas, a scion of this family, was drawn into a conspiracy against the Emperor Alexius Comnenus, and imprisoned in this tower. Anne Comnenus the historian, and her mother, induced

The Walls of Constantinople

Alexius to remit the sentence which condemned Michael Anemas and his brother to loss of eyesight, and after some years they regained their liberty.

A formidable dungeon, this Tower of Anemas, with its narrow, vaulted cells of enormous strength and its narrower passages. Others whom we know languished here in chains, among these the Emperor Andronicus Comnenus, who left this prison to die at the hands of his infuriated subjects.

Another whom we have met, Andronicus, the son of John VI Palæologus, was confined here by his father. He effected his escape, and in turn imprisoned his father and his brothers Manuel and Theodore. Perhaps the best that can be said of this rebellious son is that he did not act on the advice of Bajazet and put his prisoners to death.

A gloomy history this strong Tower of Anemas tells us. A tale of civil war, of tyranny, of deadly family feuds and the endless misery of human weakness when it is invested with some transient semblance of external power.

In strong contrast stands out that more rugged Tower of Isaac Angelus. Here it is said the Varangians, Cæsar's bodyguard, had their head-quarters, and through all the gloom that envelopes the history of the later Greek empire, the conduct of those troops

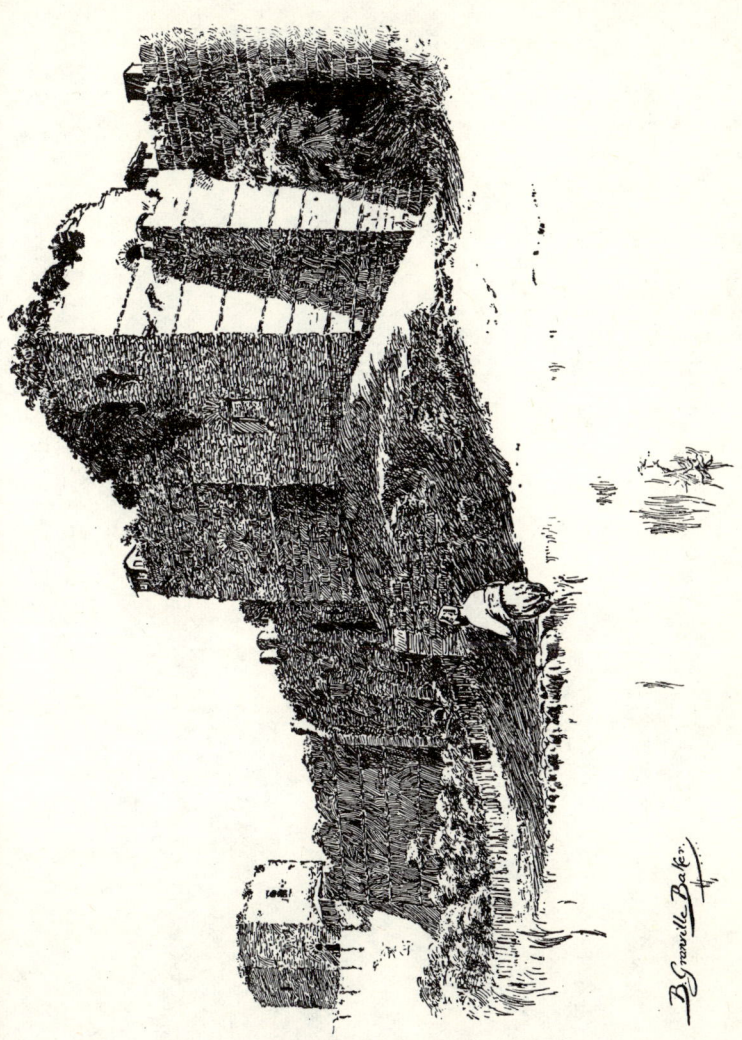

TOWERS OF ISAAC ANGELUS AND ANEMAS.

A gloomy history this strong Tower of Anemas tells us. In strong contrast stands out that more rugged Tower of Isaac Angelus.

From Gate of Edirné to Golden Horn

shines like a beacon light; the race these men sprang from was in its infancy, and they brought to the service of the Eastern Emperor the unspoilt faith and valour of a youthful nation.

The origin of the first Varangians is obscure; the name is derived from a Teutonic source, fortganger, forthgoers, men who had left their country in quest of adventure. There is reason to suppose that the first Varangians to take service with the Eastern Cæsar were of that Norman race who, so long hidden in the darkness of their northern home, suddenly burst forth upon the world as pirates. Their sharp-prowed ships first scoured the Baltic Sea, and landed these adventurous spirits on the shores inhabited by Fennic and Slavonic races. Their arms and discipline commanded respect, and by helping these Slavs against their enemies inland, the Varangians obtained the mastery over a weaker race, and gave it a succession of strong rulers. These in their turn adapted themselves to their changed circumstances, and finally a Scandinavian chief, Rurik, established a dynasty that ruled over the northern Slavs for many centuries. His descendants in time became one with their subjects and sought to check the recurring inroads of fresh Varangians. The sword of these Corsairs had raised Vladimir to the throne; the riches he had to offer in

The Walls of Constantinople

return for their services proved insufficient, so they accepted his advice and sailed back the way they came. They sallied forth out into the North Sea, and made their way to warmer climates. After many encounters with the Moors and others who followed the profitable calling of piracy, they found their way to the city of Byzas and took service with the emperors of the East.

In time the fame of this warrior's Eldorado reached other northern countries, and they too sent recruits to fill the gaps that constant warfare had torn in the ranks of the Eastern Empire's vanguard, the Varangians. So from England, so little known to the Eastern contemporaries of William the Norman that it was held to be the mythical island of Thule, came strong-limbed Saxons driven from their homes. Danes, too, were found amongst this trusted body, and their weighty battle-axes and stout hearts defended the declining Roman Empire until its death agony on that fateful 29th of May, 1453. The shadows of night are closing upon us, and here and there a light shines out through latticed windows as we turn in towards the town. The day's work is done, and here and there a figure moves silently along to disappear down some dark alley. The narrow streets are almost deserted. This is the quarter of the Phanar that we are now approaching. In former days a lighthouse

OLD HOUSE IN THE PHANAR.

Here and there we may see an old house whose stout walls have resisted all attempts at destruction.

From Gate of Edirné to Golden Horn

stood some way further on and guided the ships that had found their way into the Golden Horn after sunset. Here and there we may see an old house whose stout walls have resisted all attempts at destruction, perhaps dating back to those days when the now ruined palace of Blachernæ was a royal residence. Perhaps courtiers or high officers of State lived here, but the barred window openings and grim-visaged walls will not reveal their secrets.

We have come to our journey's end and must leave these lonely quarters for those haunts frequented by foreigners. So we will walk down to the shore of the Golden Horn. A caique is in readiness to carry us onward to the bridge of Galata. Beyond it ships ride at anchor in the stream, or are moored alongside the deserted quays. One or other of those ships will carry our travellers back into the western seas, back to those countries which owe their political existence to the walls that still encircle the City of Constantine. The city looms black against the clear sky of a southern night, and the crescent moon draws pale glints of light from the pinnacles of slender minarets. Stamboul is wrapt in darkness. On our left the lights of Galata and Pera shine out, where the Western races take their pleasure after the day's work.

The Walls of Constantinople

Behind us, by those frowning walls, a slight sound is borne upon the night wind. Its voice whispers through the branches of the many cypress-trees. It calls in gentle, insistent tones, and thousands answer by obeying it. They come from out the shadows of the broken walls, they move silently among the tumbled tombstones. Silently they mount the ramparts and gaze with serene, far-seeing eyes, out over the sleeping city. Greeks of all ages, Turks who fell before them, fearless Franks, brave Normans and stout-hearted Saxons, hold their nocturnal watch.

"The Oracle spoke true—the City prospers," whispers Byzas the founder. "It is well!"

"The descendants of the people that I loved are happy and at peace," comes from John Comnenus. "It is well!"

"The Crescent shines upon the capital of a strong Empire—the sons of Othman rule wisely," murmurs the Conqueror Mahomed. "It is well!"

The Frank looks back upon the part he played in the history of this sleeping city. His deeds were not done in vain. "It is well."

A silent group looks out over the city. Britons who followed as captives in the train of Theodosius, Normans who had camped outside the city walls under the banner of the Cross, Saxons and Danes

From Gate of Edirné to Golden Horn

who had met them in the field and on the ramparts with their battle-axes. They have followed with eager eyes the history of those that came after them. They saw the red cross of St. George's ensign float above the first ships that Queen Elizabeth had sent here. They saw that flag extended to denote the union of races that make up their nation, and watched it sail away up the narrow channel of the Bosphorus to the Crimea. These shades of departed Varangians, who fought till their last breath for an expiring cause, for an Empire whose sons had lost the art of war, have watched the rise of yet another Empire in the West in that dear land they sailed from. They have followed closely the history of that Empire, and a sigh goes from them, " Is it well ? "

ENVOI

Gentle travellers! our journey is at an end, and nothing remains to Author and Artist but the pleasant recollection of your company and the kindly interest you were pleased to show.

The sun has risen upon another day, but that is no reason why the doings of a previous one should be forgotten. The ships that bear our travellers to sea, or maybe the train on the Roumelian Railway, will soon break up a very pleasant party. So before we go let us ask you to retain a kindly memory of this journey, and of the city walls that suggested it. We ask it for a particular reason. A rumour is afloat, and has not as yet been contradicted, that these old walls are doomed, behind whose sheltering care Europe and the different nations to which you belong worked out their destiny. But for these walls what might the state of Europe be to-day? Wave after wave of Asiatic aggression here spent its fury, until in time the nation that grew up within them lost the power of defence, and accordingly ceased to be.

Envoi

But these walls still stand, if only as relics of an historic and romantic past. And they are doomed. Already the pick is at work upon the Theodosian walls, near the Palace of the Porphyrogenitus. The object is to sell the material in order to provide the army of the new Turkish Empire with means of defence and offence. But these walls have served their purpose, their stones have now no value but that to which their history entitles them.

Fellow-travellers—it may not be too late, it may yet be possible to save these landmarks that have led us through the maze of history and Romance to the present day, where with the best intentions a vigorous young government intends to inaugurate a new era by an act of vandalism.

The power of public opinion is great. Author and Artist suggest it as a means of saving the walls of an Imperial city to their friends and fellow-travellers—and so Farewell!

APPENDIX

CHRONOLOGICAL TABLE

[AUTHOR'S NOTE.]

In this table are set forth only the dates of events recorded while glancing at the history of the "Walls of Constantinople." As the book does not profess to be an exhaustive history of Constantinople, but rather a reflection of the historic happenings these Walls have witnessed—so this table aspires to do no more than guide the reader through past ages with here and there a date as milestone.

B.C.
658.	Byzas founded the city.
479.	Pausanias defeated the Persians at Platæa.
450 (about).	Xenophon born.

A.D.
306–337.	Constantine I, the Great, to whom the city owes its present name.
364–378.	Valens, whose aqueduct still stands.

Appendix

378–395.	Theodosius I, the Great, who divided the Roman Empire between his sons Arcadius and Honorius.
395–408.	Arcadius, in whose reign the Goths laid waste Greece.
404.	Eudoxia, wife of Arcadius, died.
408–450.	Theodosius II, in whose reign the Theodosian walls were built. The Greeks fought with success against Persians and Varani. Attila appeared before the walls of Constantinople and forced the Emperor to pay him tribute.
457–474.	Leo I.
518–527.	Justin.
527–565.	Justinian I, the Great. Theodora, his wife.
545.	Bertezena established Empire of Turks in Tartary.
558.	Turkish Embassy to Justinian.
610–641.	Heraclius (who executed Phocas and succeeded him).
622.	Heraclius distinguished himself in the Persian War.
626.	Unsuccessful attempt of the Avari on Constantinople.
631–641.	Arabs conquered Phœnicia, Euphrates countries, Judæa, Syria, and all Egypt.

Appendix

642.	Constans obtains the throne.
650.	Constans murders his brother Theodosius.
653.	Arabs conquered part of Africa, Cyprus and Rhodes.
668.	Constans died at Syracuse.
669.	Arabs attacked Constantinople.
685–695.	Justinian II.
695–697.	Leontius.
697–705.	Tiberius (Apsimar).
705–711.	Justinian II (restored by Bulgarians).
711–713.	Phillipicus (Bardanes).
717–740.	Leo III (the Isaurian).
740–775.	Constantine V (Copronymus) wrested part of Syria and Armenia from the Arabs; overcame the Bulgarians.
779–797.	Constantine VI.
797–802.	Irene.
802–811.	Nicephorus I forced to pay tribute to the Arabs; fell in the war against the Bulgarians.
811–813.	Michael I (Rhangabe).
813–820.	Leo V (the Armenian).
820–829.	Michael II (put Leo V to death, 826). Under his reign the Arabs conquered Sicily and Crete.

Appendix

842–867.	Michael III (confined his mother Theodora in a convent); he left the government in the hands of his uncle Bordas, and was killed by
867–886.	Basil I (the Macedonian).
886–912.	Leo VI (the Wise).
912–958.	Constantine Porphyrogenitus (his mother Zoe).
919.	Romanus Lecapenus obliged him to share the throne.
944.	Constantine and Stephanus, sons of Romanus I.
958–963.	Romanus II.
963.	Nicephorus II (Phocas) put to death
970.	by John Zimisces, who carried on an unsuccessful war against the Russians.
963–1025.	Basil II (Bulgaroktonos) vanquished the Bulgarians.
1025.	Romanus III married Zoe and became Emperor; she had him executed, and raised
1034.	Michael IV to the Throne.
1041.	Michael V.
1042.	Constantine X.
1042.	Zoe and Theodora.
1056–1057.	Michael VI, dethroned by

Appendix

1057–1059. Isaac Comnenus, who became a monk.
1059–1067. Constantine XI (Ducas), who fought successfully against the Uzes; Eudocia, his wife, entrusted with the administration
1067–1078. Married Romanus IV.
1081–1118. Alexius (Comnenus); Crusades commenced in his reign.
1118–1143. John II (Comnenus).
1143–1180. Manuel I (Comnenus).
1180–1183. Alexius II (Comnenus), dethroned by Andronicus.
1183–1185. Andronicus I, dethroned by his guardian,
1185–1195. Isaac Angelus; in turn dethroned by his brother,
1195–1203. Alexius III.
1203–1204. Alexius IV and his father Isaac restored by Crusaders.
1204. Alexius V (Ducas) put Alexius IV to death. Isaac died at the same time.
1204. The Latins conquer the city.
1204–1260. Latin Emperors (Baldwin I died in captivity in Bulgaria).
1204–1260. Nicæan Emperors (they reigned at Nicæa as Constantinople was in the hands of the Latins).

Appendix

1260–1282.	Michael VIII (Palæologus) on restoration of the Greek Empire.
1282–1328.	Andronicus II, who denounced connection with the Latin Church, which Michael VIII had restored.
1288.	Ertoghrul succeeded by Othman.
1341–1391.	John VI (Palæologus).
1342–1355.	John V (Cantacuzene).
1361.	Sultan Amurath took Adrianople.
1376–1379.	Andronicus IV (Palæologus) usurped the throne.
1391–1425.	Manuel II.
1396.	Bajazet besieged Constantinople, and defeated an army of Western warriors under Sigismund near Nicopolis.
1402.	Tamerlane's invasion of Turkish provinces in Asia saved Constantinople.
1425–1448.	John VII (Palæologus).
1444.	Amurath II extorted tribute from John VII
1451.	and died at Adrianople.
1448–1453.	Constantine XII (Palæologus).
1451–1453.	Siege of Constantinople.
1451–1481.	Mahomed the Conqueror of Constantinople.
1481–1512.	Bajazet II resigned in favour of

Appendix

1512–1520. Selim I, who murdered his brothers, proclaimed himself champion of Orthodoxy and became the first Caliph.

1520–1566. Solyman I, the Great, contemporary of Francis I of France, Charles V, German Emperor.

1526. Campaigns against the Western nations; Hungarians beaten at Mohacz.

1529. Buda-Pesth taken; siege of Vienna.

1537. Barbarossa, Solyman's admiral, conquered combined fleet of Emperor, Pope and Venetians off Prevesa.

1553. Mustapha, son of Solyman, executed in presence and by order of his father, through Roxalana's instigation.

1566–1574. Selim II.

1574–1604. Mahomed III; first English Embassy sent to the Porte.

1617. Achmet I sends Embassy to France.

1618. Mustapha I reigned six months and was deposed.

1644. Sir Thomas Bendish, English Ambassador in reign of Ibrahim, obtained justice by means of a drastic measure.

1683. Sultan Mahomed IV; siege of Vienna raised by Sobieski.

Appendix

1702.	Turkey admitted into the European system.
1707.	Achmet III allied himself with Charles XII of Sweden.
1769–1774.	Panslavism.
1774–1792.	Mustapha III. War with Catherine of Russia. Suvarrov defeated the Turks—Azov, Trebizona, Silistria and Shumea taken by Russia. The Crimea taken by Prince Potemkin.
1792–1815.	Turkey involved in Napoleonic wars.
1815–1840.	Greek rebellion. Battle of Navarino. Czar Nicholas waged war with Turkey, Kars and the Dobrutsha taken.
1854–1856.	Crimean War.
1879.	Russo-Turkish War.
1909.	Abdul Hamid deposed and constitutional Government introduced.